The Impasse of Post-Conflict Reconstruction

Economic Growth vs. Governance in Angola

Francisco Kapalo Ngongo

Strategic Book Publishing and Rights Co.

Strategic Book Publishing and Rights Co.
12620 FM 1960, Suite A4-507
Houston TX 77065
www.sbpra.com

ISBN: 978-1-61897-521-8

DEDICATION

To those who show that peace is not just the absence of conflict but the creation of an environment where all can flourish, regardless any social markers of difference.

To men and women whose task is to create the conditions in which everyone has the opportunity to create a better life for themselves

To those searching for ways to transform government from a system serving minority interests to one that meets the needs of all the people.

TABLE OF CONTENTS

FOREWORD

By Michael H. Allen

Political independence was achieved late in the countries of Southern Africa compared to others on the continent. When Angola, Mozambique, and Guinea-Bissau liberated Portugal from Fascism and themselves from the authority of Lisbon in 1974–75, most other parts of sub-Saharan Africa was formally independent for fifteen years on average, leaving only Zimbabwe, Namibia, and South Africa to establish African majority rule in the next two decades. This delay in Southern Africa came about primarily because these were colonies of settlement, as earlier in Algeria and Kenya, in contrast with most of the rest of Africa, which were used as territories for extracting strategic resources or as strategic buffers from rival empires. Where continuity of access could be achieved by handover to indigenous leadership, then European powers could accommodate decolonization by negotiation, co-optation, or ballot. Where European settlers had laid down fixed capital, extensive infrastructures, built institutions to protect and govern these, and cultivated family ties and fond memories of places to call "home," they did not give up without a fight. Hence, wars of liberation and reaction were fought in Southern Africa, including Angola, where land was critical to smallholders from an underdeveloped, though metropolitan Portugal and oil and its revenues were critical to the Portuguese government and its NATO allies.

The stakes in these wars were heightened by the alliances, technologies, discourses, and funding of the Cold War. One effect was that the nationalist movement in Angola was largely militarized from early on. With a predominantly rural agricultural African population and relatively undeveloped urban industrial and service economy at the time, the social forces upon which a deeply rooted political movement could be based were thin and dispersed. Thus, even from the beginning, the MPLA, the most politically sophisticated of the three nationalist movements—perhaps because of its urban base—was dominated by a strong elite that was at least as powerful as the base upon which it drew support. This did not bode well for the future of accountability. For its part, UNITA was even more dependent upon the personality of its charismatic and strong-willed leader, Jonas Savimbi. And to compound matters, UNITA drew its support from the southern part of the country and a different ethno-linguistic base from that of the MPLA. This was the potent brew that boiled over once the lid was suddenly lifted by the coup in Portugal. Angola went straight from liberation war to protracted civil war without the opportunity to build trans-ethnic solidarity and habits of decision-making within institutions of state, economy, and cultural reproduction.

The institutions of the state were being fought over by leaders who were used to fighting for what they wanted and to political and diplomatic mobilization as services to elite projects. If democracy is in one sense the pursuit of collective goals that are collectively arrived at under leadership that is accountable to a mandating base of support, then in terms of both habits of thinking among its elite and in terms of institutional structures of party and state, Angola began its post-colonial phase on an undemocratic footing.

That these elites were to inherit an oil enclave economy could be a blessing or a curse, improving or exacerbating the prospects for democracy as institutional habits and procedures at one level, and as realized outcomes of social and economic rights at a deeper level. That is the burden of this volume by Francisco Ngongo. With time and effort, the civil wars came to an end with the Luena Agreement of 2002. Since that time, Angola has experienced economic growth and the modernization of some of its urban infrastructures, but not development in its people-centric meaning. Ngongo helps us to distinguish growth from development, provides benchmarks for measuring both, and pointers for possible causal connections between them. Angola is yet another test case in African post-colonial performance, and the debates on this are as vigorous as the problems are complex.

The material in this book is fuel for debates on several questions: What are the forms of the post-colonial state and are they conducive to democracy and to development? Is national cohesion a precondition for democracy or can a post-colonial state construct nationhood out of the quiltworks of ethnicities left over from imperial boundaries? What is development, what are human rights, and what is the dialectic between them? Are notions of human rights universal or hegemonic, and if the latter, what conceptions of rights if any, might Africans regard as autocentric? Is development occurring in Africa? Is development occurring anywhere? Are growth and infrastructural modernization preconditions or products of development? What are the pathologies and opportunities of oil economies as one kind of export monoculture, that is, does the kind of growth and modernization oil exports facilitate, deform, or transform society as measured by human rights? Since the heritage of colonization was broadly similar across Africa and the outcomes since decolonization so varied across the continent, how are the variations to be explained? Are the failures the result of poor leadership and dysfunctional institutions, and are the apparently successful countries to be emulated by the obvious failures?

Of course, no one volume can engage all of the literatures deeply and at once. But even though Ngongo confines himself primarily to the convergence between the conversations on economic growth, development, and human rights by drawing upon the work of Amartya Sen and of the United Nations Development Program and its human development indicators pioneered by Mahbub ul Haq and others, the echoes of conversations on all the other questions are unmistakable in the background.

What is at stake in Angola is also at stake elsewhere in Southern Africa. Botswana is regarded as a success in terms of democratic forms, per-capita income, human rights, and a history of respectable leadership, but it is also an export monoculture centered on diamonds. How vulnerable are its achievements in the face of the structured dynamics of mineral dependence? What we find about oil in Angola might be helpful in Botswana despite the differences in institutions and rights. Mozambique, Zimbabwe, and in several ways, South Africa, are led by de-colonization revolutionary movements cum political parties, which, like the MPLA in Angola, became used to governing with comfortable majorities. In all those cases, the qualities or deficiencies of intra-party democracy and accountability have had direct, and in Zimbabwe, ominous consequences for democracy or the reversal of it, in state and society more broadly. We may learn much from Angola about the effects of additions or deficiencies in education, agricultural output, infrastructural modernization in transportation and communications, migration to cities, and about the impact of links with investors and trading partners in the traditional West. Emerging powers like China and Brazil who invest in and trade with Angola have been less intrusive on issues of governance and human rights. How do these effects and relationships create or forestall openings for human rights advocacy and bargaining, for example? What insights on the importance of constitutional design and the independence and professionalism of the judiciary might be drawn from the South African experience under the parliamentary dominance of the African National Congress (ANC), for analysis and advocacy in Angola? These comparative analyses are likely to be crucial to those in Southern Africa and beyond, who want to advance human welfare with sustainable production in just societies. They might offer vital insights on where to begin.

Professor Michael H. Allen
Department of Political Science and
Center for International Studies,
Bryn Mawr College,
Bryn Mawr, Pennsylvania, USA

ACKNOWLEDGMENTS

I am grateful to a number of people and organizations that supported my PhD research in the UK, which produced my thesis that is transformed into this book. First, my heartily profound gratitude and appreciation are addressed to my supervisor, Dr. Fiona Macaulay for her encouragement, help, and kind support. Her invaluable technical and editorial advice, suggestions, discussions, and guidance were a real support to complete my PhD thesis.

I would also like to acknowledge financial support provided by the Karl Popper Zug Foundation (Switzerland) that enabled me to cover my living expenses in the United Kingdom and my fieldwork in Angola. I am thankful to the British Council for paying my tuition fees through its Chevening Scholarship Program. My special thanks go to Sir John Tompson, the former British Ambassador in Angola, for paying special consideration to my application for the Chevening Scholarship. My thesis would not have materialized but for the help of Dr. Cornelio Sommaruga, former President of Red Cross. As a friend and as a mentor, he has helped me continuously and encourages me throughout difficulties. I consider it as my fortune to be his friend.

Particular thanks go to my research participants (members of political parties, government officials, civil society, embassies, international organizations, and United Nations agencies) who, despite their tight schedules, have taken part in my interview sessions. To my English-speaking friends, who instead of their multiple occupations read parts of my thesis and corrected the spelling errors. To those whose names are not mentioned here, I ask their sincere forgiveness and say many thanks to all for your kind assistance and contributions that made a success of this PhD thesis.

I. INTRODUCTION

Often the signing of a peace agreement that ends violence in a country gives hope that the government will deliver and the majority of the population will benefit from a peace dividend. However, in the real world, this hope can be transformed into a myth or reality. What can be learned from economic growth and human poverty after ten years of cease-fire in Angola? The book builds on the PhD thesis that I successfully defended in 2008 at the University of Bradford's Peace Studies Department, in the UK; I analyzed the correlation between the macroeconomic situation and living conditions of people in post-conflict Angola. It explores the extent to which political factors influence human development in post-conflict Angola. I discuss issues related to post-war economic strategies and distribution of wealth.

The twenty-seven years of civil war ravaged the economy, disturbed social order, and disrupted social stability. This posed a major challenge to human development in the post-conflict setting. The situation in Angola changed considerably during 2002, when the two belligerent parties, the Popular Liberation Movement of Angola (MPLA) and the Union for the Total Independence of Angola (UNITA), signed a comprehensive cease-fire agreement, the Luena Memorandum of Understanding. Since then, Angola has been experiencing a high economic growth rate.

Nonetheless, the post-war atmosphere in Angola is one of mixed perspectives. On the one hand, there is great hope that the human development of Angolans will be sustainable as the country's economic indicators have drastically improved.[1] On the other hand, there is the challenge of transforming the country's economic growth into sustainable human development. Therefore, I analyze the extent to which poverty in Angola persists and what can be done to promote sustainable human development in post-conflict this country.

The book is crucial in that it provides a detailed and critical study of human development in post-conflict Angola, which has so far been overlooked in the existing academic literature. It makes specific contributions to the literatures in fields of (1) economics, due to the fact that it demonstrates the extent to which economic factors are not the sole determinants of human development using the case of Angola; (2) governance, as it presents key socioeconomic variables that are vital for government policies to boost human development analysis; and (3) human rights, as it shows the extent to which a rights-based approach is useful in the analysis of human development and the impact of economic performance on people's living conditions.

Both economic and social variables should be included in the causalities of human development. I have used Sen's "capability approach"[2] and the United Nations Development Program (UNDP)'s "rights-based approach"[3] to analyze data on human development in post-2002 cease-fire Angola. The combination of the two approaches is fruitful as it enables me to assess the interface between economic and social factors. Moreover, reference to these approaches enabled me to design a framework for analysis of human development data that comprises basic civil and political as well as socioeconomic rights.

The UNDP's Human Development Index (HDI) has been criticized on a number of grounds. The index fails to include any ecological considerations and does not reflect political participation or gender inequality. Therefore, the approach proposed in this book is much more comprehensive, as it encompasses additional variables that are not included in the measurement of the UNDP's Human Development Index.

I have used a triangulation methodology combining both quantitative and qualitative methods[4] in order to consolidate the validity of the data analyzed. The use of this methodology has enabled me to deepen and widen the interpretation of the results. I have used information collected during fieldwork in Angola and secondary data from well-reputed organizations, such as the Angolan parliament, the UNDP, and the World Bank. Survey data has been used to produce a quantitative representation of the research participants' perceptions about the nature of human development in post-conflict Angola. Data from interviews, informal conversations, and secondary sources has been used to provide a broader and more critical discussion of the results. The data analyzed in this book was regularly updated whenever new information was acquired.

This chapter gives a brief historical and structural context of the late Cold-War, liberation wars in Southern Africa, the unique circumstances in Angola that led to a protracted civil war, the Accords that ended the conflict, and the forms of state and party leadership that are to be found in Southern Africa and Angola in particular. Then it raises the issue that human development is not occurring in Angola despite economic growth having been enabled by the post-conflict Accords and oil money. It shows why it makes sense to criticize such non-development in light of the synthesis developed by combining Sen's notion of Capabilities and the UNDP's concept of Human Development. It contracts UNDP's HDI with World Bank/IMF notions of GDP growth. It introduces the notion of Welfare Democracy that is discussed in the Conclusion of the book as recommendation.

1.1. Historical Factors Influencing Human Development in Angola

Angola was a Portuguese colony from the Fifteenth century, when Diego Cão arrived in the Kingdom of Congo[5] in 1482. We can regard the struggle for independence in Angola and other African countries as the quest for the "right to self-determination."[6] The independence movement further accelerated following United Nations General Assembly Resolution 1514 of December 1960 that clearly stipulated the right for independence of African countries.[7]

As in other African countries, the struggle for independence in Angola was initiated by a small number of educated elites eager to fight colonial power and defend the overall objective: the "right to self-determination" of African people. The desire for independence and popular resentment against racism, labor exploitation, and inequality imposed by the colonial regimes were the main causes for the creation of liberation movements. These movements transformed themselves into political parties after independence (Birmingham 1995). The social contract during the struggle for independence was that liberation movements would overcome colonial power and form a national government capable of restoring human dignity.

Many African people believed that colonial powers would be defeated and their countries would be governed by national elites who would promote and protect their fundamental rights and promote sustainable development. But this is a myth for many African countries, including Angola, where the living conditions further deteriorated following independence. In order to understand the African struggles for independence, it is useful to refer to Trotsky's[8] analysis of the Chinese revolution. The type of bourgeois nationalism that developed in China in 1927 became the political inspiration of the future Pan-Africanist leaders, who later established the regimes in post-Colonial Africa (Kunnie 2000).

The Portuguese colonization and decolonization processes in Africa were significantly different from those of other Metropolitan powers (Chabal 2002). During the late 1950s and early 1960s, when many African countries began to gain independence from their colonial powers, Portugal was not prepared to transfer authority to its African colonies and continued to consider them overseas provinces and integral parts of the Portuguese State (Black 1992).

Portuguese colonial policies in Africa had remained in breach of the 1885 Berlin Conference Agreement on the occupation of Africa (Chabal 2002). The suppression of the Angolan people by the Portuguese was affected first by conquest and thereafter by the settlement of the metropolitan Portuguese on their land. Angolan people were dispossessed of their land and forced into contract labor under harsh conditions (Makidi-Ku-Ntima 1983). A large number of Portuguese traders, missionaries, soldiers, and criminals arrived, settling and oppressing Angolan people (Adedeji 1999). Hence, during colonial time, Angolan people were deprived of their human dignity and development.

Outraged by the brutality of Portuguese colonial power, the first anti-colonialism movements constructed themselves in the mid-1950s.[9] In December 1956, the Angolan Communist Party (PCA), the Party of the United Struggle for Africans in Angola (PLUA), and other left-wing-oriented organizations united as one and formed the Popular Movement for the Liberation of Angola (MPLA).[10] The other liberation movements were the National Front for the Liberation of Angola (FNLA) formed in 1957 and the National Union for Total Independence of Angola (UNITA) formed in 1966. The first goal of the creation of these liberation movements was to retaliate against

Portuguese colonial atrocities and to ultimately win independence and restore human dignity among Angolan people.

Throughout the struggle for liberation in Angola, the three liberation movements engaged in violent hostilities among themselves. Competition for post-independence power was the major organizational goal of the Angolan liberation movements. There was no compromise as to who would be the president of Angola after the independence. Each of the leaders of the liberation movements wanted to be president. Their focus was on searching for ways and means to win the presidency of the country after the independence. Each of the three proclaimed he was the true representative of Angolan people. From this, we saw that the military and financial support requested to defend the independence of Angolan people was later deployed into the power struggle between the leaders of the three liberations movements, jeopardizing the true vision of the struggle for independence (Tahri 2007).

Economic factors motivated Portugal to fight Angolan nationalism and contributed to the prolonged liberation struggle in Angola (Okuma 1962, 137). Portugal, under Salazar,[11] instituted an economic system that was designed to exploit the colonies for the benefit of Portugal by excluding or strictly limiting foreign investment. Nonetheless, by April 1965, Portugal faced increasing defense expenditures in order to resist the growing military strength of the nationalist movements. This forced Salazar to permit the influx of foreign capital, which resulted in rapid economic growth in Angola (Bender 1972).

The 1974 coup d'état in Portugal that overthrew Salazar's authoritarian regime was the doorstep for independence in all Portuguese colonies in Africa (Burchett 1978).[12] After fourteen years of struggle for independence, and following months of negotiations, the first comprehensive cease-fire between the Portuguese colonial army and the three liberation movements eventually took place (Birmingham 1993). Accordingly, in January 1975, a pro-independence agreement for Angola, known as the Alvor Agreement, was signed in Alvor, Portugal (Gjerstad 1976).

The agreement entailed the creation of a transitional government with a Portuguese high commissioner and collegiums of presidency from the three principal liberation movements: twelve ministries divided equally among the four parties (FNLA, MPLA, UNITA, and Portugal) and the formation of a new national army (Birmingham

1992). Furthermore, the transitional government was to organize the election as a constituent assembly by the end of October 1975, with candidates chosen from the three movements. This assembly would produce a new constitution (Gjerstad 1976).

However, the parties did not fully respect the Alvor Agreement due to mistrust and continued competing for post-independence power. With growing backing from Cuba and the Soviet Union, the MPLA managed to push the FNLA and UNITA out of Luanda (Gjerstad 1976). Accordingly, despite all the confusion surrounding the aftermath of the Alvor Agreement, the MPLA proclaimed independence on November 11, 1975, and its leader, Agustinho Neto, was recognized as the first president of the Angolan single-party government[13] (Spinola 1974, Somerville 1986).

1.1.1. Civil War and Cold War Geopolitics

Despite Portugal's decision to grant Angola its independence, the differences between the FNLA, MPLA, and UNITA had not yet been resolved. By January 1976, with the support of Cuban troops and Soviet arms, the MPLA had emerged as the sole dominant military power in Angola (Somerville 1986). After it came to power, the responsibility to restore the human dignity and development of the Angolan people lay with the MPLA and its leader, President Neto.

Although the MPLA gained control of Angola's central government, UNITA and FNLA refused to recognize MPLA's authority. Civil war between the three movements of liberation continued following the proclamation of independence by the MPLA. The FNLA and its mercenaries were defeated in northern Angola, leaving UNITA as the only formal military opposition to the MPLA government. With the Soviet Union and Cuba supporting the MPLA, and the United States and South Africa supporting UNITA, the country became a Cold War battleground (Black 1992).

The interference of superpowers in Angola began during the struggle for independence. The United States thought that if the MPLA gained power through its strong connection with Cuba, there would be the first physical penetration of the Eastern bloc into African affairs. The United States regarded that as a strategic treat. In addition to the United States, the South African apartheid regime was also determined to fight the MPLA, as well as its allies—Cuba and the Soviet Union—in Angola. The South African apartheid regime considered communism a threat. Accordingly, the South African defense force decided to move into Angola with the mission to reach Luanda and put UNITA in power (Gjerstad 1976). Cuba (a key Soviet ally) and South Africa's apartheid (a US ally) troops continued to fight within Angolan territory after independence.

The Cuban and the South African apartheid regimes played critical roles in post-colonial Angola. Although Cuban and South African intervention in Angola was a war of ideology, they both claimed to fight to establish a kind of democratic government that would be able to sustain human development in the country. While Cubans supported the MPLA socialist model of government, the South Africans supported UNITA to defeat the MPLA and establish a pro-Western liberal regime (Gleijeses 2003).

However, there was a contrast between what ideas the two countries intended to implement in Angola and the democratic performance of their governments. Neither Cubans nor South Africans were democratic at home. Cuba implemented a non-representational regime while succeeding in improving the welfare of people through redistribution of wealth (Halebsky et al. 1992). Cuba supported the communist idea of Leninism, which opposes capitalism and defends social justice (George 2005). Critics could argue that despite Cuba having a well-organized and developed welfare system, the majority of Cuban people were still deprived of their fundamental freedoms (Human Rights Watch website, 2006).

Although Cuba helped the MPLA and its leadership stay in power, it was difficult for the MPLA government to reproduce the Cuban welfare approach. This is because the government's efforts were much more focused on winning the war against UNITA and not so much on promoting the welfare of people. The South African coalition with UNITA gave the Cubans an excuse to stay in Angola and protect the MPLA. Hence, the MPLA's leadership justified a strong and unchallengeable rule as a response to South Africa-UNITA's aggression. The promotion of the well-being of people is the key aspect of human development, but this cannot be sustained if people are not able to enjoy their fundamental freedoms. Therefore, one can assert that Cuba's intervention in Angola contributed little to sustaining human development, but it did enable MPLA to consolidate its power and resist aggressions, as well as develop a defensive posture to resist the United States.

South Africa's involvement in post-independence Angola increased because of the situation in neighboring Namibia, where the insurgent group the South West Africa People's Organization (SWAPO) received support from the MPLA government. The main objectives of South Africa were to maintain control in Namibia and fight communism in Angola. The South African apartheid regime's claim that they were a representative democracy was contentious, as the multiparty elections at home were reserved for the white minority and excluded the black population.

Therefore, the claim by the South African apartheid regime that it intended to bring democracy to Angola was disputable. The South African apartheid regime was in grave breach of democratic human rights: impeding the right to self-determination of the Namibian people; oppressing the majority of the South African and other African populations; arresting thousands of pro-democratic voices, including the distinguished Nelson Mandela (Asmal, Chidester, and James 2003). Hence, it is difficult to believe that such a brutal regime could help UNITA to implement a democratic regime and sustain human development in Angola.

The intervention of both Cuba and the South African apartheid regime in Angola was politically motivated. Neither Cuba nor the South African apartheid regime supported a genuine human development idea in Angola. The renewal of civil war, as well as Cuba's and South Africa's interventions in Angola, obstructed the premise for the post-colonial government to provide services for human development. Following independence, the MPLA government did not have any time to settle in as the war began. As its large budget spending was allocated to war efforts, there was less money to invest in rebuilding social infrastructures. In addition, it was practically impossible for the government to set up a program for national reconstruction during wartime as each belligerent party was occupying part of the country. Moreover, the state of war allowed the MPLA to justify a single-party authoritarian regime.

1.1.2. Post-Colonial Political Development

Following independence in Angola, the MPLA's leader, Antonio Agostinho Neto, became president of Angola and stayed in power until his death in 1979. President Neto spent his four years in power fighting the war against the UNITA rebellion and dealing with Cold War geopolitics. The death of President Neto on September 10, 1979 did not present any panic or vacuum within the camp of the MPLA, nor did it present an opportunity for UNITA to advance more quickly to Luanda. On December 20 of the same year, the MPLA's Central Committee held a meeting where President Jose Eduardo dos Santos[14] was chosen as the Neto's successor (Wolfers 1979).

The war against UNITA and the US geopolitics continued to pose challenges to MPLA and its new leader. President José Eduardo dos Santos came into power when the superpower conflict in Vietnam ended. Angola marked a new era of Cold War confrontation, with a new site for conflict between the United States and the Soviet Union (Meijer and Birmingham 2004). In 1980, less than one year after the induction of President José Eduardo dos Santos into power, Ronald Reagan was elected president of the United States. This election was one of the critical external junctures for Angolan politics. Reagan's vision of the Cold War was to alter the course of events in Southern Africa (Tahri 2007). As Herman Cohen attests, President Reagan's strategy was to do anything within his power to counter the Soviets as well as to take revenge on the Soviet Union for what it had done to the United States in Vietnam (Tahri 2007). Angola was seen as perfect place to take revenge as there were Soviet advisers, Cuban troops, and a pro-Soviet government.[15]

In 1987, the MPLA army was losing its war against UNITA and facing a large number of causalities. As a result, Cuba decided to send their best anti-aircraft batteries, aircraft, armored units and artillery to Angola. During this time, Russian–Cuban relations were tense. Mikhail Gorbachev's rise to power had radically changed the Soviets' priority toward the Third World and toward Angola in particular (Brown 2006). However, with the support of Cuba, President Dos Santos' regime continued to strongly oppose UNITA aggression.

Decreasing Soviet interest in Angola stimulated the Cuba-MPLA coalition to change their approach and opt for a peace negotiation with UNITA. Accordingly, on September 29, 1988, Reagan and Gorbachev agreed to withdraw foreign troops from Angola—the end of the Soviet military aid to Angola—as soon as South Africa pulled out from Namibia (Rothchild and Hartzell 1991). On December 12, almost one month before the end of Reagan's presidency, a peace accord was signed in New York. The parties simultaneously signed documents granting Namibia its independence and ensuring the withdrawal of foreign troops in Angola. At President dos Santos' and Fidel Castro's request, the first United Nations Angola Verification Mission (UNAVEM I) was established by Security Council Resolution 626 of December 20 (UN Security Council 1988).

Since 1989, there have been several attempts by the two belligerent parties to achieve a cease-fire. A solution became easier when the MPLA decided to give up Marxism-Leninism and the one-party state. An agreement was reached in 1991 on a new constitution, the merging of the two rival armies, and the holding of multiparty elections. The end of the Cold War opened an opportunity for initiating a democratic political change. Hence, on May 31, 1991, the MPLA and UNITA signed the Bicesse Accord in Lisbon, Portugal, under the supervision of Portugal, the United States, and the Union of Soviet Socialist Republics. This accord laid the foundation for the abolition of the MPLA's one-party system, the transformation of UNITA from a rebellion movement to a peaceful political party (Birmingham 1999). Furthermore, the accord set provisions for the demilitarization of both MPLA and UNITA soldiers, the formation of a single army, and the holding of the first multiparty elections.[16] Accordingly, civil society organizations, independent media, and opposition parties began to operate after the signing of the Bicesse peace agreement. The signing of the Bicesse Accord raised hope concerning the formation a democratic government capable of sustaining human development in Angola.

The key political factors that affected the MPLA government's incapacity to deliver services for human development prior to the Bicesse peace agreement are the civil war between MPLA and UNITA, the Cold War geopolitics, and the single-party regime. The atrocities of the civil war further destroyed the already poor socioeconomic infrastructures left by the Portuguese and enhanced widespread human poverty. Instead of helping the two belligerent units (MPLA and UNITA) to solve their differences, Cuban and South African presence only seemed to worsen the situation. At the time, the MPLA profited from the conflict situation and used its Leninist ideology to implement a single party that suppressed people's political rights and basic freedoms.

Data on political parties in Africa show that at the end of the Cold War, forty-one African countries were ruled by single-party systems.[17]

However, when the wave of multiparty elections reached Africa, more than half of these single parties were replaced with newly elected parties. The MPLA was among the nineteen single parties who managed to cope with the wave of change and continued to control political power. Analysts and scholars argue that there has been rise of dominant party systems, which pose huge challenges to the idea of building institutions for good governance and human development in some African countries (Bogaards 2004; Joseph 2004; Ottaway 1997).

Generally, multiparty elections are one of the important components of a peace building and functioning democratic system. Elections open an opportunity for people to choose their legislatures and leaders. Therefore, it can be argued that the 1992 elections were a test for Angolan political actors to resolve their differences and build a new era of prosperity and good governance. The result of the legislative elections was uncontested by opposition parties, and the MPLA won the majority of votes.

Angola used two round systems for the presidential election in 1992. Eleven candidates participated in the 1992 Angolan presidential elections. However, as shown in Table 1.1, none of the candidates managed to secure the minimum of 50 percent required by the Angolan constitution in order to be declared a winner. Accordingly, a runoff was supposed to take place between the two best candidates: President José Eduardo dos Santos of the MPLA and Jonas Malheiro Savimbi of UNITA.

Table 1.1. Summary of the 29 and 30 September 1992 Angola presidential election results

Candidate	Party	Votes	%
José Eduardo dos Santos	MPLA	1,953,335	49.57
Jonas Malheiro Savimbi	UNITA	1,579,298	40.07
Antonio Alberto Neto	ADP	85,249	2.16
Holden Roberto	FNLA	83,135	2.11
Others		700,322	6.09
Total		4,401,339	100

Source: Compiled from Adam Carr's Election Archive, the African Elections Database and Onofre dos Santos (1992). The table is in descending order according to each party's number/percentage of votes. The last row above the total represents the percentage of other candidates who each achieved less than 2% of votes including invalid and blank votes.

Despite international observers assuring that the first round of elections were fair, while the country was waiting for the second round of the presidential election, Dr. Savimbi rejected all the results and resumed war. UNITA asked for a complete rerun of elections, proposing a transitional government in which it would have equal influence with the MPLA government and refusing any meeting between Dr. Savimbi and President José Eduardo dos Santos (Brittain 1993). As a result, the UN Security Council in its resolutions 804 of January 20, 1993; 811 of the March 12, 1993; and 834 of June 1, 1993 adjusted the mandate of the UNAVEM II. The United Nations mission was extended in order to help the two parties to reach an agreement and, at the same time, to broker and help implement cease-fires.

The renewal of conflict between Dr. Savimbi and President José Eduardo dos Santos enormously damaged both people's lives and any hope of building institutions of good governance. Thousands were killed during this period, there were many assassinations of alleged members of UNITA by MPLA supporters, tens of thousands of impoverished people fled from UNITA-occupied towns and villages, and substantial economic damage was done by UNITA's extensive destruction of dams, factories, homes, and offices (Brittain 1993).

Moreover, UNITA's decision to resume war was a huge political and diplomatic mistake that negatively affected the direction of the party. Abroad, UNITA lost credibility and was under permanent pressure from members of the international community. At home, the renewal of war gave the MPLA leadership an opportunity to regain political power. Although the dominance of the MPLA in the National Assembly was justifiable, as it was the party that had won the majority of the votes in the 1992 election, the authority of the president was questionable because of a lack of a second round of presidential elections.

There have been discussions by members of the international community, opposition parties, and civil society over the longevity, legality, and legitimacy of dos Santos' mandate. Some argue that the president did not achieve the minimum percentage of votes in the 1992 and, therefore, should not have stayed in power. Others say President José Eduardo dos Santos had a moral justification to cover the vacuum of power after Savimbi's rejection of elections results that were considered to have been free and fair. The scenario of the post-1992 era was quite similar to that of the post-1975 period, where the state leadership took authoritarian measures to resist opposition. Savimbi's refusal to recognize Neto's authority provoked an immediate civil war after the Angolan independence in 1975. Similarly, the refusal by Savimbi to recognize the result of the 1992 elections permitted the continuation of civil war in Angola in the post-Cold War era.

The state of war gave moral justification for the MPLA leadership to stay in power and control the political direction of Angola. When the war erupted in 1992, President dos Santos was forming a new government, of which 20 percent were members of peaceful parliamentary opposition parties (Black 1992; Brittain 1993). However, the inclusion of the non-MPLA members in the government was just a symbolic gesture as they did not have enough say in the decision-making process. Moreover, it was difficult to question the MPLA's policies or its leadership given the fact that the country was in a state of war.

On May 19, 1993, the United States (which backed UNITA between 1975 and 1991) recognized the MPLA government and José Eduardo dos Santos as the legitimate leader of Angola. The shifting of sides by the US government weakened UNITA's military strategy. Moreover, UNITA was under unprecedented diplomatic and military pressure, as the end of apartheid in South Africa and the coming into power the African National Congress (ANC) in 1994 removed its last significant source of external support.

Despite widespread condemnation by members of the international community, UNITA continued its insurgency against the MPLA government. Having lost its firm international allies (United States and South Africa), UNITA continued to be armed by private security groups. Moreover, during that time, UNITA relied on revenues from the illicit trade of diamonds to buy weaponry and sustain its rebellion. In order to persuade UNITA to abandon violence and agree to enter peace agreements, the UN Security Council imposed more sanctions on the former. In the meantime, the MPLA regained its international and national recognition as the legitimate government. As a result, it continued to consolidate its dominance in power.

The civil war after the elections was even more violent than the post-independence war. During two years of fighting, it was calculated that some two million people were driven away from their homes (20 percent of the population). More than 20 million land mines were planted by the warring factions. Moreover, the MPLA government found it difficult to improve the economic conditions during that time due to huge social disruption caused by the intensive fighting (OCHA 2004).

Organized economic activity was largely restrained to the main towns, under government control, and the coastal oil-producing sector, as most infrastructure and trading systems inland were destroyed by the years of war. This particularly affected diamond output, as the main producing fields have been under UNITA control since early 1993. The value of illegal diamond production by UNITA and individual diggers was running at some $30m annually. In contrast, production from government-controlled areas had fallen from 1.4m carats worth some $270m in 1992 to under 200,000 carats last year. Coffee, once Angola's biggest export, had suffered a similar precipitous decline as most plantations were in a poor state or in areas still controlled by UNITA (Global Witness 2000). Furthermore, Angola had an expanding budget deficit, mainly due to diversion of oil resources to maintain the MPLA's military capacity, rampant inflation, and a deteriorating balance of payments (IMF reports). As a result, it was difficult to sustain human development in the country, as there was less investment in building socioeconomic infrastructure and institutions for good governance.

1.1.3. Breach of Peace Agreements

In conflict societies, a peace agreement is a very important instrument, as it is the turning point from conflict to a peace-building process. Respecting peace agreements can help the prosperity of society, and its breach can turn the society to another violent conflict. Therefore, stakeholders should pay attention to the regulations set out in the peace agreement in order to consolidate peace and sustain human development. Nevertheless, Angola has a history of broken peace-agreements that led to violent conflicts and a deterioration of living conditions of people.

Failure to observe the Avord agreements made it difficult for leaders of the three liberation movements to decide who should rule the country after the departure of the Portuguese. This led to the post-independence civil war between the MPLA and UNITA. From 1989 on, there were several attempts by the two belligerent parties to achieve a cease-fire. However, UNITA's rejection of the 1992 election results jeopardized the success of the Bicesse Accord, therefore allowing the continuation of civil war in post-Cold War Angola.

UNITA's adamant conduct and rejection of the national reconciliation package proposed by the MPLA government increasingly frustrated the United States. As a result, the United States backed the UN Security Council sanctions on UNITA. Meanwhile, the MPLA was launching a counter offensive to deprive UNITA of much of the territory gained since the beginning of the post-elections war. As a result, in 1994 the MPLA government troops captured UNITA's stronghold of Huambo. The military success of the MPLA government's forces obliged UNITA to agree to a cease-fire and engage in negotiation with dos Santos' government (Krška 1997). Accordingly, on November 20, 1994, MPLA and UNITA representatives signed another cease-fire agreement in the Zambian capital city Lusaka, known as the Lusaka Protocol. The protocol provided a cease-fire, formation of a unified army and police force, formation of a government of national unity (GURN), and the disarmament and transformation of UNITA from rebellion movement to a political party (Lusaka Protocal 1994).

The key political issues stipulated in the Lusaka Protocol were the UN mandate for verification and monitoring of the Lusaka Protocol, the role of peacekeepers, the completion of the electoral process, and national reconciliation. UNITA was also to hold a series of posts as ministers, deputy ministers, ambassadors, provincial governors and deputy governors, municipal administrators and deputy administrators, and district administrators. The government would retain all other key positions. The GURN was inaugurated on April 1997, and this included members of the MPLA, UNITA, and the ten other parliamentary parties. As a result, the UN Security Council in its Resolution 1118 of June 30, 1997 established the United Nations Observer Mission in Angola (MONUA) to replace the UNAVEM III. The overall mandate was to assist the Angolan parties in consolidating peace and national reconciliation, enhancing confidence-building and creating an environment conducive to long-term stability, democratic development, and rehabilitation of the country. However, the protocol was continuously violated by both MPLA and UNITA, and the UN mission was much criticized for being passive (CIDCM 2005).

Despite the formation of the GURN and the reinstatement of the National Assembly, the MPLA continued to dominate policy making and implementation as it achieved the majority of members in the National Assembly. Despite the international community's acknowledgement that both sides were violating the Lusaka agreements, UNITA was blamed with much more intent for not disarming in the first place. Accordingly, in August 1998, the MPLA government suspended participation by UNITA members in both the National Assembly and the GURN (Messiant 2004). Hence, in December 1998, there were full-scale hostilities across much of the country.

UNITA's leader no longer enjoyed the full sympathy and external bilateral support that he had during the Cold War era; he relied on diamond revenues to finance his war.[18] Since 1992, UNITA had consistently controlled about 70 percent of Angola's diamond production, generating US$ 3.7 billion in revenue, enabling them to maintain their war against the MPLA government (Alley and Yearsley 1999). By early 1999, UNITA was in control of large part of the Angolan territory. However, in late 1999, an enormous military offensive led by the Angolan armed forces severely destabilized the military capacity of UNITA (CIDCM 2005).

In October 1999, some UNITA parliamentarians formed a faction, known as UNITA-Renovado (Cornwell 1999). The leader of UNITA-Renovado, Eugenio Manuvakola, called for international intervention to bring an end to Angola's civil war, saying that "the UNITA members who collaborated in good faith with this policy were betrayed by Dr. Savimbi" (Malaquias 2000). Accordingly, the MPLA chose to cooperate with the UNITA-Renovado while pursuing its war against Savimbi's rebellion. Critics argue UNITA-Renovado was strategically supported by the MPLA as a way to weaken UNITA and its leader Savimbi (Malaquias 2000).

Following the death of Dr. Savimbi, the Angolan government and UNITA signed the Luena Memorandum of Understanding on April 4, 2002. This agreement recognized an immediate cease-fire and called for UNITA's return to the agreements laid out in the 1994 Lusaka Protocol.[19] However, having lost the war, UNITA lacked the capacity to challenge the MPLA. Furthermore, the death of Savimbi left a leadership vacuum within UNITA, which enabled the MPLA to consolidate its dominance.

1.2. Understanding of Human Development

An analysis of the state of human development in post-conflict Angola first requires a better understanding of its definition and how it is deployed in this book. The human development approach arose in part because of growing criticism to the leading development approach of the 1980s, which presumed a close link between national economic growth and the expansion of individual human choices. The work by Sen (1999) and the UNDP (1990) provide the conceptual foundation for an alternative as well as a broader human development approach. They describe human development as a process of enlarging people's choices and enhancing human capabilities and freedoms (Sen 2001). Hence, in order to enlarge these choices, building human capability is essential to enable people to fulfill their basic needs (Kuklys 2005).

In 1990, the UNDP launched the first Human Development Report (HDR) with the fundamental goal of putting people back at the center of the development process in terms of economic debate, policy and advocacy. Since the first report, four new composite indices for human development have been developed: the Human Development Index, the Gender-related Development Index, the Gender Empowerment Measure, and the Human Poverty Index. Each report also focuses on a highly topical theme in the current development debate, providing ground-breaking analyses and policy recommendations. The reports' messages and the tools to implement them have been embraced by people around the world, as evidenced by the publication of national human development reports at country level in more than 140 nations (UNDP 2006).

The working definition of human development in this book is drawn from Sen's and the UNDP's approaches. Hence, human development in this book is defined as the process of creating an environment in which people have the capacity to develop their full potential and enjoy their lives in accordance with their fundamental human rights. This working definition has enabled me to examine the correlation between Angolan post-conflict economic growth and people's living conditions using a rights-based approach. Hence, the book makes a valuable contribution to the existing literary and operational discussions of HDI. The conceptual framework proposed in the book can be used in other human development case-studies.

1.2.1. Conceptual Framework

The conceptual framework has been developed by relating the rights-based and capability approaches to human development. In recent years, international efforts to deal with development issues have increasingly been using human rights-based approaches. The links between human development and human rights, and attempts to redefine human development as a normative conception grounded in the human rights doctrine, have had growing support. Human development and human rights are mutually reinforcing, helping to secure the well-being and dignity of all people—building self-respect and the respect of others (VeneKlasen 2004).

Human rights-based approaches to development have been formulated and are being tested out in a period of neo-liberal globalization (Endreassen 2008). They have grown out of human-centered approaches to development in the 1990s, responding to the challenges posed by contemporary processes of globalization to resolve fundamental problems of subsistence and security, social injustice, political oppression, recurring high levels of poverty, marginalization, and social exclusion. The fact that at present more than one billion people live in severe poverty demonstrates that international human rights politics and law enforcement are still far from achieving their goal of ensuring people's basic human rights to subsistence, participation, and security (Endreassen 2008).

A human rights-based approach constitutes a holistic framework methodology with the potential to produce an operational strategy for human development. It adds a missing component to present activities by empowering people to make their own decisions and by enabling equitable development. The human rights-based approach brings in legal tools and institutions under the judiciary and the rule of law principle as a means to secure freedoms and human development (UNDP 2001). It is further based on the recognition that real success in tackling poverty and vulnerability requires giving the poor a chance, a voice. and real protection in the societies in which they live (Jahan 2002).

Poverty is generally now understood as a result of disempowerment and exclusion, which means taking away people's capacity to choose their life style and enjoy their fundamental human dignity. The human rights approach is used in the analysis of both poverty reduction and human development paradigms.[20] Fighting poverty and sustaining human development require the promotion of civil and political rights (CPR) as well as economic, social, and cultural rights (ESCR). I have regrouped these human rights into six, which are used in this book to analyze data of people's living conditions in post-conflict Angola. As shown in Table 1.2, these rights are freedom of association, freedom of expression, freedom of movement, right to health, right to work, and right to education.

Table 1.2. Basic Human Rights Pertinent to Human Development

Basic Rights	Indicators
Freedom of Association	Freedom to form and run an organization (opposition party, civil society organization, religious organization, syndicate movement)
Freedom of Expression	Freedom to express political opinion, free media, free political campaign...
Freedom of Movement	Availability and accessibility of infrastructure, safety in the streets, transport, building bridges, clearing landmines...
Right to Health	Availability and accessibility of medical infrastructure, food, water, hygiene, elimination of pollution, equal opportunity, access to health...
Right to Work	Work conditions (reasonable salary, none exploitation), fight unemployment, equal opportunity in jobs....
Right to Education	Availability and accessibility of educational infrastructure (training centres, schools, universities), equal opportunity in education, affordable fees

Source: Author

Table 1.2 illustrates that for each category of basic rights pertinent to human development there are different indicators. The mechanism for the promotion and protection of these rights differ from one society to another. For example, while freedom of movement in peaceful societies may require doing things such as tracking down street crimes and maintaining roads, in a post-conflict society, it may include clearing land mines and rebuilding bridges and roads. People need to have both economic and political capabilities in order to be able to enjoy their basic human rights, which are relevant to human development. For example, while people need economic empowerment to be able to do things such as buy food, pay bills, and travel, they need protection to be provided by their government so that there is a secure environment for them to fulfill their needs.

1.2.2. Economic Growth for Human Development

The major problem explored in this book is why despite almost ten years of economic growth after the conflict in Angola, the country is still one of the poorest in the world. The analysis of economic factors enables the analysis of the extent to which economic growth poses a potential threat to Angola in sustaining human development. Economic growth, however, is a means and not a goal for promoting human development (Ranis et al. 1997). To be useful, economic growth must be able to provide people with the ability to satisfy their needs and interests. The first major attempt to translate Sen's capabilities approach into a ranking of nations came in the 1990 UNDP Human Development Report. The report's objective was to have a better understanding of the complexity of human life by providing a quantitative approach to combining various socioeconomic indicators into a measure of human development. This was in contrast to the perceived existing knowledge in development economics, as stipulated in the World Development Reports,[21] whose excessive concerns with gross national product (GNP) growth and national income accounts have replaced a focus on end-results with an obsession with merely the means (Shalizi 2003).

Income growth may clearly be considered as the main contributing factor to directly increasing the capabilities of people and consequently the human development of a nation since it indicates the economy's command over resources (Sen 2001). GDP may have a strong effect on literacy and health outcomes, both through private expenditure and government programs. The impact of economic growth on a government's human development expenditure is bound to supplement private expenditure channels.

As Anand and Ravallion (1993) demonstrate, most of the effects of economic growth on human development are likely to flow through government budgetary expenditure. However, the influence of these effects depends completely on the effectiveness of government expenditure. The government needs to identify priority sectors such as primary education and health, which have the highest potential for improving human development. Accordingly, the promotion and protection of basic human rights may enable the government to sustain human development (Aturupane, Glewwe, and Isenman 1994).

The promotion of certain socioeconomic and cultural human rights may be achieved only progressively due to legitimate resource constraints. For example, rebuilding socioeconomic infrastructures in a post-conflict society may take a long time depending on available resources and political willingness. However, under internationally binding regulations, states have an obligation to take measures to realize these human rights as quickly as possible. Since resources are needed to realize these particular rights, their prompt realization depends on improving the resource constraint, which in turn needs economic growth. Hence, a faster growing economy can also help ease the pain of building or sustaining socioeconomic infrastructures by increasing available resources (Ranis and Stewart 2006).

However, it is important to mention that ensuring faster growth is one thing and connecting its potential for the cause of human development is another. For economic growth to lead to the realization of human development, any growth strategy must be part of a comprehensive set of policies and institutions consciously designed to convert resources into rights (Shalizi 2003). Government expenditures for human development should be distributed mainly to low income groups and regions since it is here that the highest marginal impact will be achieved. Governments must also have the institutional capacity to efficiently allocate these expenditures. Studies by Rajkumar and Swaroop (2002) have demonstrated that the effectiveness of public expenditure is conditional on the quality of governance, with government accountability likely to play an important role. In summary, the analysis of economic factors in this book enables us to explore the correlation between economic growth and human development.

1.3. Political Factors of Human Development

Analysis of political factors enables exploration of the quality of governance and its effects on human development. Governance refers to mechanisms, institutions, and processes through which authority is exercised in the conduct of public affairs. Accordingly, the concepts "state leadership" and "party system" are crucial to the analysis of governance, as the former guides and the latter forms the government. The behaviors of state leaders and the ruling parties have major implications for human development. When ruling elites act in favor of good governance, human development has a high chance of improving (Smith 2007).

Dahl (1991) considered a multiparty democracy as a political institution that tends to produce the best feasible system of good governance. Existing literature has developed various arguments that link democracy to good governance (Abdellatif 2003). A number of multilateral organizations, including the UNDP and the World Bank, have reflected on the elements of good governance and on their relation to democracy (Newman and Rich 2004). The establishment of good governance institutions may also produce practical benefits for citizens. Such benefits may come in various forms: better protection of human rights, less corruption in the government, and greater economic prosperity (Leftwich 1993; Edozie 2006).

The term good governance emerged in the late 1980s to address failures in development policies due to governance concerns, including failure to observe human rights. Developing the capacity for good governance can be a prerequisite for eradicating poverty. However, notions of good governance and the link between governance and human development vary significantly both in academic literature and among development practitioners (Wohlmuth 1998).

Marxist and socialist thinkers who argue that liberal democracy is an integral part of the capitalist system and is class-based and not participatory attacked multiparty democracy or liberal democracy (Haberler 1981). Hence, opposite to the liberal democracy was the

Soviet or Cuban model, the one-party democratic socialism. This model advocated the idea that poverty, oppression, and exploitation were a result of control of the world's wealth by imperial power[22] (Fitzpatrick 2003).

Empirical studies prove that democracy correlates with a higher score on the human development index and a lower score on the human poverty index. Democratic governments tend to put in place better education, longer life expectancy, lower infant mortality, access to drinking water, and better health care than authoritarian systems. This is not due to higher levels of foreign assistance or spending a larger percentage of GDP on health and education but is due to good management of available resources (Halperin, Siegle, and Weinstein 2005). Several social indicators such as health and education have a stronger and more significant association with democracy than they have with GDP per capita, size of the public sector, or income inequality. Moreover, Sen (2001) argues that no functioning democracy has ever suffered a large-scale famine or refugee crises.[23]

Amartya Sen (1994) observes that the rights promoted and protected under democratic institutions can considerably improve the well-being of citizens. It can be argued that consolidating democratic institutions of good governance, which fosters political competition and public participation, can facilitate the fight against corruption that usually provokes a poor human security (Sen 2001). There is evidence that countries with higher degrees of civil liberties are found to have less corrupt governments (Pei 2001). Hence, democratic values of human security and good governance encourage the institutional checks and balances that prevent the massive hijack of public wealth often observed in autocracies (Olson 1993; Weingast 1997; Scully 1998)

The notions of good governance and human rights are initially reinforcing as they are both based on core principles of participation, accountability, transparency, and government responsibility (Sano and Alfredsson 2002). Human rights necessitate a favorable environment, in particular suitable regulations, institutions, and procedures outlining limits to the actions of the government. Human rights provide a set of performance standards against which governments and other actors can be held accountable. At the same time, good governance policies should empower individuals to live with dignity and freedom.

Although human rights empower people, they cannot be observed and protected in a sustainable way without good governance. In addition to relevant laws, political, managerial, and administrative processes and institutions are also needed to respond to the rights and needs of citizens. To demonstrate a good government, ruling elites need to support mechanisms for people to exercise control, not only over the decision making but also over the decision makers who act on their behalf (O'Donnell 1994; Schedler, Diamond, and Plattner 1999). They must be both promoters and protectors of people's basic human rights.

With multiparty elections being conducted in many part of the world, the state is generally directed by an elected government and an executive branch. There are state various functions (Edwards 1970) including: (1) a state is the focus of the social contract that defines citizenship, (2) it is the authority that has mandate to control and exert force, and (3) it has responsibility for public services and creating an enabling environment for sustainable human development (Hvid and Hasle 2003).

The latter means: (a) establishing and maintaining stable, effective, and fair legal-regulatory frameworks for public and private activity; (b) ensuring stability and equity in the market place; (c) mediating interests for the public good; and (d) providing effective and accountable public services.

In all four roles, the state faces a challenge of ensuring that good governance addresses the concerns and needs of the poorest by increasing the opportunities for people to seek, achieve, and sustain the kind of life they aspire to (UNDP 1994). The government can do much in these areas, such as upholding the rights of the weak, protecting the environment, maintaining stable macroeconomic conditions, and maintaining standards of public health and safety for all at an affordable cost. It must mobilize resources to provide essential public services and infrastructure as well as maintaining order, security, and social harmony (Wilson, Kanji, and Braathen 2001).

Government institutions must empower the people they are meant to represent by providing equal opportunities, as well as by ensuring social, economic, and political inclusion and access to resources (UNDP 1994). However, people can be empowered only if their legislatures, electoral processes, and legal and judicial systems work properly. Parliaments of freely and fairly elected members representing different parties are crucial to popular participation and government accountability. Effective legal and judicial systems protect the rule of law and the rights of all. Open elections mean public confidence and trust—and so political legitimacy. States should also decentralize political and economic systems to be more responsive to citizens' demands and to changing economic conditions.

Existing literature has developed various arguments that link democracy to good governance (Abdellatif 2003). It is true, as it has been said that "democracy is the worst form of government except all the others that have been tried" (Quinault 1979). There will always be problems and complaints about how the government works. There will never be a perfect government, and some will always disagree with the way societies are governed. However, if democratic principles of participation and equality in politics are observed, it is possible to find compromises and people's consent over government policies.

A number of multilateral organizations, including the UNPD and the World Bank, have reflected on the element of good governance, and on their relation to democracy (Newman and Rich 2004). The establishment of good governance institutions may also produce practical benefits for citizens. Such benefits may come in various forms: better protection of human rights, less corruption in government, and greater economic prosperity (Leftwich 1993).

It important to bear in mind that Sen's discourse of consolidating democratic institutions of good governance as perquisite for human development is more normative than dialectical, and that is its weakness. It presumes a small amount of democracy that can be used to build more democracy and human capabilities. But where do you begin when hegemonic control is almost absolute, as in Angola?

Appeals to human rights obligations in the Angolan constitution and treaties, naming and shaming by intergovernmental bodies, and democratic education at grassroots level are good. But what of the independent power of the courts in Angola, in contrast to Botswana and South Africa? Can Angolans bring suit against their government in terms of human rights and achieve anything? Can they gain access to international government institutions and still travel freely at home? Can think tanks and universities be credible crucibles of democratic education? Can they penetrate the grassroots organs of the MPLA? Can the educational strategy transcend ethnic suspicions so that the MPLA does not interpret it as UNITA propaganda and so discredit it?

Thus, Chapter VI, "Conclusion and Policy Implication," refers to the notion of welfare democracy to complement the UNDP's rights-based approach to development and Sen's capability approach.

As Fitzpatrick (2003) summarized, welfare democracy involves an attempt to maximize social justice through strategies of empowerment. Welfare democracy is initially about the realization of basic needs and about a collective, democratic quest whose value resides in the fact that the expedition is endless. Therefore, democratization in Angola should go together with the process of building credible and durable state institutions capable of promoting people's well-being.

While it is widely believed that multiparty competition influences the democratic decision-making process, there has been relatively little effort to examine the link between the democratization process in Angola and human development. There have been even fewer attempts to investigate whether democratization matters for public spending in Angola, where "weak institutions" may mean that the formal adoption of multiparty competition has little effect on policy. Therefore, directly asking whether the democratization process in Angola is a prerequisite for promotion of human development is crucial. Furthermore, the discussion here shows the extent to which democratic stagnation makes it difficult to promote human development in post-conflict Angola.

Analyzing political factors can illustrate how the Angolan government has responded to the need to promote and protect basic rights that are the bedrock of sustainable human development. It has also enabled analyzing how the behaviors of state leadership and the ruling party in Angola affect the government's ability to deliver services for human development.

1.4. Analysis of Human Development in Post-conflict Angola

The concept of human development occupies a predominant position in the international realm. In Africa, where poverty is at an alarming point, the analysis of human development should be considered as a key of indicator for understanding the government's performance in delivering services, the efficiency of investment and aid, as well as the degree of people's happiness. Poor human development can be caused by either natural hazards, such as droughts and tsunamis, or by human action, such as war and corruption. Although the government is the main party responsible for promoting human development, it needs full support from others stakeholders, mainly the people it represents and members of the international community.

In order to elaborate on a critical analysis of human development, I refer both to primary and secondary data. The primary data analyzed in this book emanates from fieldwork conducted in Angola from May 10, 2004 to July 23, 2004 and from May 3, 2005 to November 4, 2005, as well as during my post-graduate work in Angola from February 2009 to April 2010. The aim of this fieldwork was to conduct primary research that enabled me to collect views from ordinary people, government officials, members of civil society, and expatriates concerning issues related to human development and human rights in Angola.

The primary data was analyzed using the responses to 116 questionnaires, content analysis of official documents collected, notes of informal conversations, and interpretation of transcripts of twenty-three semi-structured interviews conducted during the fieldwork in Angola. The analysis of the fieldwork data is both quantitative and qualitative. This use of a triangulation approach allows a full explanation of the features and challenges of human development in Angola by studying it from more than one standpoint. Hence, *The Impasse of Post-Conflict Reconstruction* presents a detailed and balanced explanation of challenges and features of human development in Angola. The techniques for data collection used were questionnaires, semi-structured interviews, informal conversations, and document exploration.[24]

The questionnaire survey was used in order to collect the views of research participants on conditions of basic human rights and human development in Angola. As shown in Figure 1.1, the sample of research population was divided into two geographic regions: the coastal and the countryside regions. Most of the respondents to the questionnaire were selected randomly among participants at four major conferences related to post-conflict in Angola. One conference was held in London in November 2002,[25] and the other three were held in Luanda, Angola, in May 2004,[26] June 2004,[27] and November 2005.[28] However, the sample was relevant and representative as it was elite-based. Moreover, participants in conferences consisted of delegations from each of the eighteen Angolan provinces.

The respondents were selected from three categories of research population: coastal, countryside, and expatriate categories. The aim was to find out what the research participants thought about the state of human development in post-conflict Angola. Therefore, the fieldwork questionnaires consisted of three subjects. The first was about the general perceptions of the post-conflict era in Angola. The second dealt with the analysis of basic human rights and human development. The third element consisted of a critical analysis of strategies used by the MPLA government to retain power.

The objective of the preliminary fieldwork conducted in Angola in 2004 was to find out how people experienced the aftermath of the conflict. Is human development condition sustaining or deteriorating? In addition to informal conversations with citizens in the city of Luanda, some key members of parliament, government, UN specialized agencies, civil societies, and diplomats and journalists were interviewed. The aim of the second period of fieldwork in 2005 was to investigate the views of key stakeholders (government officials, members of parliament and political parties, diplomats, members of international and domestic civil society) in Angola about the condition of fundamental rights relevant to human development in Angola. Finally, during my stay in Luanda from 2009 to 2010, I was able to deepen my understanding of the complexity of post-conflict reconstruction of Angola and reflect on the pertinence of publishing this book.

Overall, the fieldwork consisted of twenty-three semi-structured interviews with members of political parties and ministers. It should be acknowledged that the interviews were primarily elite led, while informal discussions with other stakeholders were used as a means for a broader understanding of the issues related to the research. Accordingly, the following research population was interviewed:

1. Members of the ruling party (including three ministers) to understand their justification for governmental policies and to explore how far they are willing to construct and consolidate institutions capable of sustaining human development in post-war Angola.
2 Members of the National Assembly to discover their views and perspectives about human development in Angola.
3. Leaders of twelve opposition parties with seats in parliament to explore their view about the problems of human development in Angola and to discover how they view the role of ruling elites in the process of sustaining human development.
4. UN agencies to find out concrete challenges the organization is facing in the effort of supporting the process of sustaining human development in Angola.
5. Representatives of international and local civil society organizations to discover their imprecations/criticisms about the nature of governance and human development in Angola.

Informal conversations were used during the fieldwork and stay in Angola, through which it was possible to ascertain the general feelings of the situation in the country. The informal conversations were mainly searching for issues related to the enjoyment of basic human rights relevant to sustainable human development.

The categories of primary documents collected during the fieldwork and which forms part of the analysis are:

1. State official documents: Peace agreement documents, the national constitution, and other legal documents were collected in order to analyze the advantages and weaknesses they present for the process of sustaining human development.
2. Newspapers:[29] The information obtained from newspapers complements the fieldwork findings.
3. The MPLA archive: Party's status, programs, and manifestos were collected. The content analysis of these documents

enabled the study to discover the correlation between what the MPLA says it ought to do and the outcome of its government policies.

4. Publications by others researchers: Articles, books, and reports of other scholars and activists were consulted. This enabled the study to review their works and bring a positive contribution to the discussion of human development in Angola.

I reviewed literature on Angolan politics, democratization in Africa, human development, human rights, party systems, and political leadership. Works such as those by Spence (2007), Chabal (2002), Webber (1992) and Marcum (1969) enabled me to discuss the political background of Angola prior to 2002. Birmingham (2006, 132-184) describes the Angola post-colonial historical background from 1975 to 2000. Chapter five of Tony Hodges' book, *Angola: Anatomy of an Oil State* (2004) was pertinent to my study as it analyses the problems of economic governance, including entrenched elite interests, the use of patronage as an instrument for the preservation of presidential power, and inadequate transparency and accountability in management of public resources. Publications such as those by Dahl (1991), Sen (2001), and the United Nations Development Program (UNDP) allowed me to explain the extent to which democratic systems are likely to promote human development.

In order to find further insights into the contrasts of post-conflict Angola, I analyzed data from the International Monetary Fund (IMF), Transparency International, the World Bank, the media, and the UN specialized agencies and treaties. The techniques for data analysis used in this study were the Statistical Package for the Social Sciences (SPSS), interpretation, and "content analysis."[30] The use of SPSS permits the study to categorize and quantify data collected into tables. Qualitative explanation is produced through content analysis of documents collected, as well as through interpretation of interview transcripts and field notes.

The triangulation method enabled me to cross-check data from different sources and search for regularities.[31] The quantitative approach enabled me to explore the scope of indicators of basic human rights pertinent to human development. The qualitative approach permitted me to explain why the political factors, not the economic factors, have had a critical effect on the process of sustaining human development in post-conflict Angola. To sum up, while the quantitative methods enable this study to represent the effects of variables analyzed, the qualitative methods help to identify their causalities and relations. Therefore, the use of the triangulation method increased the credibility and validity of the study results.

Ethical issues were observed during the fieldwork. This includes the right of interviewees to withdraw from the research investigation at any point if they wished to, the right to refuse to answer any question asked, and the right to remain anonymous and to have the confidentiality of their data protected. Angolan legislation and academic standards on ethical issues were analyzed.

Interviewees were free to give their consent to being involved in my research investigation. Letters stating the objective of the fieldwork and the contact details of the researcher were sent to the interviewees prior to the interview sessions. This permitted them to decide whether to take part in interview sessions. In the case of the questionnaire survey, participants were asked for their authorization to answer the questions.

The research data was stored in a secure manner and appropriate methods for preserving anonymity and confidentiality were taken. The names of interviewees are not revealed to anybody, except in anonymous forms in the book. Furthermore, the research information was used for the purpose of this research; no part of the data collected was to be re-used by people for other research or non-research purposes.

As a social science researcher, I had responsibility not to expose the research participants to any potential harm. It is important to notice that the concept "harm" does not only refer to physical damage but also to psychological harm and embarrassment. Therefore, precaution has been taken not to use any word that could cause distress. Regarding physical well-being, one of the main dangers in Angola is land mines. Even though the fieldwork was mostly based in Luanda, visits to the province of Moxico, where there are still widespread anti-personal mines, were made. Accordingly, to avoid risk, before visiting any place in the countryside, safety information from local people and organizations dealing with land mines were consulted.

The book consists of six chapters. This introduction chapter gives readers a brief historical-structural context of the late Cold War and liberation wars in Southern Africa, the unique circumstances in Angola that led to a protracted civil war, the Accords that ended the conflict, and the forms of state and party leadership that are to be found in Southern Africa as well as in Angola in particular. It introduces the problem that human development is not occurring in Angola despite economic growth enabled by the post-conflict Accords and oil money.

This chapter shows why it makes sense to criticize non-development in Angola in light of the synthesis I have developed combining Sen's notion of Capabilities and the UNDP's concept and indicators of Human Development, using Human Development Index (HDI) in addition to/contrast with World Bank/IMF notions of GDP growth. It is here that I introduce my notion of Welfare Democracy that is further discussed in the Conclusion chapter of the book. In addition, the introduction outlines what the driving forces behind social/economic/political change generally are and how the structural/ historical legacies channel how these flow and create the outcomes I describe in Angola.

From Chapters II to V, *The Impasse of Post-conflict Reconstruction* provides readers with an account of how far Angola has gone, its failings, and what still needs to do as measured by the Sen/UN criteria. This is a good employment of mixed data-driven analysis based on field surveys and qualitative/normative analysis. This tells non-specialists in the region what is going on and also allows specialists on other African and Southern African countries to compare notes and critiques in a detailed and empirically supported way.

Chapter II provides empirical evidence of human development in post-conflict Angola based on primary and secondary data collected. It triangulates quantitative and qualitative data in order to produce an analytical explanation of the condition of freedoms of association, expression, and movement as well as rights to health, work, and education. The findings show that the conditions of these basic rights are poor, which reflects the prevalence of human poverty in post-conflict Angola.

Chapter III analyses the macroeconomic situation of Angola in the post-conflict period. It explores how much capacity Angola has to address people's basic needs. The first section analyses the economic wealth in post-conflict Angola, looking at the country's national output. This has enabled me to analyze the extent to which the Angolan economy has the potential to contribute to rapid growth and sustainable human development. The second section assesses some deficiencies of economic performance and doing business in post-conflict Angola.

Chapter IV analyses the correlation between macroeconomic and human development in Angola. The first section analyses the contrast between rapid economic growth in Angola and human poverty. It assesses the impasse of post-conflict economic growth and explores issues related to the "resource curve" theory. The second section explores the prospects for sustainable human development in post-conflict Angola. It analyses the responsibilities of key stakeholders for sustainable human development in Angola. It raises some policy recommendations that would enable the Angolan government, academic institutions, and members of civil society and the international community to combine their efforts for the promotion of sustainable human development in post-conflict Angola.

Chapter V explains the extent to which the heart of Angola's problem lies in the undemocratic nature of the ruling party, MPLA, and not only because it is a dominant party. In this chapter, the book compares Angola to other Southern African countries; it explores the fact that Botswana's and South Africa's structures are similar as post-colonial forms of state and ponders over the differences in their dynamics. Chapter six concludes the book. It is here that I explore the notion of why welfare democracy matters, especially with regards to the promotion of human development in post-conflict Angola.

Summary

By analyzing Angola's political background, I have explained the key factors that contributed to the poor human development in Angola prior to the 2002 cease-fire. The chapter discussed different Angolan political processes that were separated by four critical junctures the Angolan politics went through. The Angolan political process began with the struggle for independence. Portuguese colonial legacy had a negative impact on human development in Angola. Hence, the creation of the liberation movement was a noble action. It aimed to end Portuguese exploitation and rebuild the human dignity of the Angolan people.

The declaration of independence in 1975 was the first critical juncture of Angolan politics, as this opened an opportunity for Angolan people to be governed by national leaders. However, the state of human development continued to deteriorate following the declaration of the independence of Angola by the MPLA in 1975, due to the continuation of civil war and Cold War geopolitics. Angola had experienced forty-one years of inter-connected wars. The twenty-seven years of interrupted civil wars between the MPLA government and UNITA rebellion had further worsen the economic situation. War produced organized violence that had direct and indirect effects on living conditions, as it led to social dislocations and the disruption of welfare. These consequences contributed to poor human development in Angola

The Cold War geopolitics contributed to the aggravation of civil war in Angola. The West-East support and the presence of Cuban and South African troops in Angola fortified the two warring parties and made the prospect for peace very difficult. Hence, the struggle to gain and maintain political power became the major preoccupation of the leaders of confronting parties while human development continued to be neglected. As a result, the MPLA government found it difficult to sustain human development as it responded to UNITA's aggression and searched for strategies to maintain power.

The end of the Cold War and the signing of the Bicesse Accords marked a second critical juncture in Angolan politics. There was hope that with the creation of a multiparty system, the newly elected government would govern democratically and build institutions for sustainable human development. However, Dr. Savimbi's rejection of the first round of the 1992 presidential elections results led to the renewal of civil war between the MPLA and UNITA in the aftermath and wiped away the hope for sustaining human development. The post-Cold War civil war, mainly after the collapse of the Lusaka agreement, was very destructive, as UNITA adopted guerrilla tactics, which indiscriminately targeted civilians and social infrastructures. Moreover, the state of war enabled the MPLA and its leader to consolidate their dominance in power. Before 2002, any critics against

Angolan ruling elites were severely punished, as they were considered as anti-revolutionary or pro-UNITA. The MPLA had the monopoly in the decision-making process, and its leadership was not accountable, either horizontally or vertically. Hence, this political situation, which lacked checks and balances, further contributed to the government's incapability of complying with democratic principles and promoting human development.

The third critical juncture was the signing of the Luena Memorandum of Understanding in 2002, as this marked a beginning of a formal peace process in Angola. The civil war between the MPLA and UNITA and the legacy of MPLA's single party and later dominant party made it difficult to build institutions capable of sustaining human development post-colonial Angola prior to 2002. After decades of war, the 2002 peace agreement made the fourth critical juncture as it presented an opportunity to restart the process of democratization in Angola. The dominance of the MPLA and President José Eduardo dos Santos in power was a common denominator of different waves of the Angolan post-colonial politics. This is why the following chapters analyze how these political variables, dominant party, and dominant state leadership influence human development in post-conflict Angola.

II. THE STATE OF LIVING CONDITIONS IN POST-CONFLICT ANGOLA

The war largely contributed to poor human development in post-colonial Angola. Hence, the 2002 cease-fire presented an opportunity to restart the process of sustaining human development. Accordingly, this chapter provides empirical evidence of human development in post-conflict Angola based on primary and secondary data. While the first section of this chapter analyses the nature of civil and political rights, the second section assesses the condition of economic, social, and cultural rights in post-conflict Angola.

According to existing indicators, Angola is still one of the poorest countries in the world; it is ranked 146 out of 169 on the UNDP's Human Development index in 2010. The impact of gender inequality on poverty in Angola is also evident, as reflected in lower human development indicators for women than men. With a lack of human security still an everyday reality, women and children comprise the most vulnerable groups. Some customary laws, however, may work against women in their efforts to become economically independent. Despite the fact that the war is over, Angolan women face new challenges as they struggle to overcome these obstacles and participate fully in society.[32] Therefore, gender issues are incorporated in the discussion throughout the book.

2.1. Civil Political Right

Promoting and protecting fundamental freedoms of association, expression, and movement is core to human development. Sen (2000) explores the relationship between freedom and development and the ways in which freedom is both a basic constituent of development in itself and an enabling key to other aspects. He analyses the relationships between justice, freedom, and responsibility. Thus, referring to Sen's

Theory, promoting fundamental freedoms is crucial for building sustainable human development in post-conflict Angola.

Sen reiterates the advantages of capabilities over narrower measures of human development. The idea of "human capital" is a step forward, but is still too narrow in its restriction to effects on production—it fails to confine the direct contribution of human capabilities to well-being and their indirect effects on social change. Hence, rather than the common focus on income and wealth, or on mental satisfaction (by utilitarian[33]) or processes (by libertarians[34]), Sen suggests focusing on substantive human freedoms (capabilities). He argues in favor of a broad view of freedom, one that encompasses both processes and opportunities, and for recognition of the heterogeneity of the distinct components of freedom (Sen 2001).

Economic needs are considered by some to be more important than political freedoms; however, Sen considers this view to be illusory. He points out that democracy, as well as being an end in itself, plays an instrumental role in giving people a voice and a constructive role in shaping values and norms. Political rights, including freedom of expression, association, and movement, are not only pivotal in inducing social responses to economic needs, they are also central to the conceptualization of economic needs themselves.

The state of war encouraged the two belligerent parties in Angola (MPLA and UNITA) to pay less attention to the protection of freedoms of expression and association in their occupied territories. Since the end of war, however, there have been some encouraging efforts in Angola toward the promotion of these fundamental freedoms. The signing of the Bicesse Accord was a step toward the promotion and protection of political rights, which encompass fundamental freedoms of expression and association. The official authorization of civil society, independent media, and opposition parties to operate on Angolan soil was an encouraging gesture for these fundamental freedoms.

2.1.1. Freedom of Expression

Freedom of expression is the right for everyone to be able to speak freely without unlawful restriction. Freedom of expression has a long history that predates modern international human rights instruments.

It is recognized as a human right under Article 19 of the Universal Declaration of Human Rights (UDHR) and recognized in international human rights law under Article 19 of the ICCPR. It is obvious that the right to freedom of expression is not absolute in any country, and it is commonly subject to limitations. This is because exercising freedom of expression always takes place within a context of competing values. However, unlawful limitations of freedom of expression can undermine the process of building democratic governance susceptible to sustainable human development. As shown in Table 2.1, in order to have an in-depth understanding of the condition of freedom of expression in post-conflict Angola, I asked my research participants to answer seven questions that explore their views on freedom to express their political views and access to media.

The first question was to find whether or not the Angolan government is doing enough to promote freedom of expression. Angola is a member of a number of international treaties that guarantee the right to freedom of expression and freedom of association, including the CCPR[35] and the African Charter on Human and Peoples' Rights.[36] These binding treaties require state parties to ensure and respect the right to receive information and express and disseminate opinions, the right to free association, the right not to be compelled to join an association, and the right to free assembly.

Table 2.1 Issues over Freedom of Expression* Origin Crosstabulation

Questions/Response categories		Respondents			Total
		Coastal	Countryside	Expatriate	
Are Angolan people free to express their political opinions in public places?	Yes	10	3	4	17
	No	44	43	12	99
	Total	54	46	16	116
How often do you read the Journal de Angola?	Often	44	13	16	73
	Not often	10	33	-	43
	Total	54	46	16	116

Questions/Response categories		Respondents			Total
		Coastal	Countryside	Expatriate	
How often do you read private newspapers?	Often	27	11	16	54
	Not often	24	29	-	53
	Not at all	3	6	-	9
	Total	54	46	16	116
How often do you listen to TPA news?	Often	50	41	16	107
	Not often	4	5	-	9
	Total	54	46	16	116
How often do you listen to private news?	Often	29	13	9	51
	Not often	13	21	7	41
	Not at all	12	12	-	24
	Total	54	46	16	116
Does the government authorise demonstrations?	Easily	11	2	16	29
	Not easily	38	10	-	48
	Not at all	5	34	-	39
	Total	54	46	16	116
Is the government doing enough to promote your freedom of expression?	No	54	45	16	103
	N/A	2	1	-	3
	Total	54	46	16	116

As Angola ratified the ICCPR on August 8, 1992, with no reservation (OHCHR 2007), it is compelled under the international regulations to implement freedom of expression. The enjoyment of freedom of expression will enable people to express their views freely, independent media to operate adequately, and opposition parties to conduct their electoral campaign freely, giving people the ability to participate in decision-making processes and contribute to the process of building democratic governance in the post-conflict era.

Although Articles 32(1) and 35 of the Angolan Constitution stipulate the right to freedom of expression, the majority of respondents criticized the Angolan government for not doing enough to promote and protect it. Women in particular found it difficult to enjoy their freedom of expression prior to and after the 2002 cease-fire in Angola. Like in many other conflict situations, Angolan women were excluded from participating fully in political life and in the formal peace negotiations between the warring parties. Neither the MPLA's women's branch, the Organization of Angolan Women (Organização da Mulher Angolana—OMA), nor the UNITA's women wing, Independent League for Angolan Women (LIMA), were able to play effective roles in bringing an end to the war. Both during and since the end of the war, Angolan women have been in constant negotiation with the political leadership, campaigning for their concerns to be taken seriously by policy makers and government officials.

The second question was to find out the opportunities people have to articulate opinions in the public sphere without fear of being persecuted. When people are able to speak without fear, they have a better chance to enjoy the right to political participation. This right can take many forms, the most prominent of which is voting in elections, including joining a political party, standing as a candidate in an election, joining a civil society organization, and taking part in demonstrations. However, the majority of respondents said that Angolan people find it difficult to express their political opinion in public freely.

The Angolan government has been opening up and tolerates some sort of freedom of expression. The minority of respondents who said they can freely express their views are mostly from the coastal region. However, the situation in the countryside is completely different, as citizens are absolutely not allowed to express their political opinion. A member of UNITA said, "Angola is undergoing two waves of democratization—democracy of the coastal part where freedom has been slightly promoted and democracy of the countryside where people are completely oppressed" (Unattributed interview 2004).

Human Rights Watch (HRW) and other human rights organizations have repeatedly demonstrated that despite some improvement in freedom of expression (mainly in Luanda and other coastal regions) in the countryside, the situation remains troubling. Opposition activists continue to be the target of violence by the police, the army, the Civil

Defense Organization (ODC), and supporters of the MPLA government. Private media is almost unknown. The judicial system does not have the independence to enforce the legislation that should in practice guarantee basic freedoms. The police force has not yet begun to fulfill its mandate as a politically neutral keeper of law and order (HRW 2004, 2007).

During my fieldwork, in Moxico province people secretly told me that they were unable to judge the government's performance because that would be considered a political offense and could have enormous political consequences. Some of them said that they were forced to take the MPLA's membership, and those belonging to other politically parties faced threats. To make things worse, the governor of the province was both a provincial secretary of the MPLA in Moxico and one of the generals of the FAA. Hence, critics[37] have said that instead of fulfilling his responsibility to govern the people in the province, the governor was more interested in political propaganda and defending his party, the MPLA.

Women's freedom to express their views and participate in political affairs is not yet well promoted in Angola. In the past, OMA played a decisive role as a policy-driven outfit dedicated to fighting for the improvement of women's legal status, as well as for their economic empowerment, and above all, the integration of women's issues into mainstream policies.[38] However, OMA's close ties to the MPLA have contributed to undermining its public credibility (Ducados 2004).

The Angolan government has been criticized for deliberately delaying or refusing to provide citizens, mainly returnees,[39] with identity documents that would enable them to get access to social services (HRW 2003). Moreover, despite the provision of Article 28 of the Angolan constitution giving Angolans over age eighteen the right to vote, many Angolans cannot practice this democratic right, since many of them are finding it hard to get identification documents and proceed with electoral registration; therefore they cannot vote.

Preventing people from exercising their political right to vote is a violation of the democratic right of expression as set forth in Article 28 of the Angolan Constitution and Article 5(1) of the 2005 Angolan electoral law. This situation jeopardized the fairness of the 2008 legislative elections in Angola.[40] As many Angolan people are still hesitant about discussing their political opinions during the pre-election period, it is very difficult for them to choose their representatives freely and fairly. Therefore, the president of the Social

Renewal Party (Partido Renovador Social-PRS) was quite right to accuse the MPLA of engaging in pre-emptive corruption and abuse during the 2008 legislative elections (Nkondo 2005).

Providing potential Angolan voters with identity documents is one of the most basic pre-conditions for the elections. However, while the Ministry of Justice started a nationwide free civil registration campaign in April 2005, it has faced serious logistical constraints. The fact is that if Angolan people cannot vote freely and fairly, it will remain difficult for them to participate in the decision-making process to improve living conditions.

The holding of the 2008 legislative elections was one of the positive steps toward the promotion of freedom of expression in Angola. Although international and national observers observed some irregularities, they agreed upon the fact that the elections were relatively free and fair. The organization of regular free and fair elections will be a positive step in the attempt of promoting freedom of expression, as these will enable people to manifest their will and choose their representatives freely. However, despite positive steps that have been taken, many more efforts are needed in order to consolidate institutions for the promotion of freedoms of expression and association.

For example, there is a need to work on areas such as promoting the right to demonstration, which is an important component of fundamental freedoms of expression. The right of demonstration could have begun in the post-Bicesse era with the start of democratic political change, but it was obstructed by the country's state of war that followed the 1992 multiparty elections. Holding a demonstration is useful in democratic society as it enables people to raise awareness of certain problems that the society is having and to seek protection from their government.

The new constitution guarantees freedom of assembly and peaceful demonstration, and Angolan laws explicitly allows public demonstrations without the need to obtain government authorization. However, although Article 32 of the Angolan Constitution stipulates that "freedom of demonstration shall be guaranteed," the whole idea is new phenomena in Angolan real-politics. The law requires a written notification to the local administrator three days before a public or private demonstration or meeting is held. Applications for pro-government assemblies usually are granted without delay; however, applications for protesters or opposition parties are often denied, usually based on government's claims that the timing or venue requested was problematic, as stated by a representative of a human rights organization.

Human rights observers and activists continue to accuse Angolan authorities of arbitrarily banning public demonstrations organized by civil society organizations, publicly threatening demonstrators, and deploying security forces to prevent the demonstrations. For example, in March 2010, a demonstration against mass forced evictions and demolition of houses in Huila, organized by the human rights organization Omunga, was banned by the governor of province. The governor deployed hundreds of police agents and publicly rejected "any responsibility" for the resulting physical damage or harm to the protesters. The demonstration later took place in April 2010 following local and international pressure.

In May 2010, the governor of Cabinda banned a public demonstration organized by civil society groups in solidarity with civilians jailed on suspicion of state security crimes after the January 8 guerrilla attack. The governor deployed the police and military to prevent the demonstration from taking place on May 22. The military and police also surrounded the organizers' houses on the day of the demonstration, despite the demonstration being called off (HRW 2010).

International human rights organizations' findings in post-conflict Angola show that the media environment in Angola remains restrictive, and the government continues to limit access to information. The freedom of the press and media in general is crucial for building and consolidating a democratic system. However, despite the fact that Article 35 of the Angolan constitution states that "freedom of press shall be guaranteed and may not be subject to any censorship," the majority of Angolan people do not have access to impartial news. Independent journalists are often intimidated, dismissed, and sanctioned by authorities (HRW 2006). Despite the emergence of a number of new media outlets since the end of conflict in 2002, the government imposes a strong political bias in the state media.

In 2010, HRW accused Angolan authorities of routinely limiting the access of private media to official information and of curtailing space for open political debate on state and private radio stations, particularly in the provinces. Authorities have also obstructed media coverage of politically sensitive events, such as forced evictions. On November 4, 2010, the parliament passed a revised law on crimes against the security of the state, which contained provisions that restrict freedom of expression, for example by declaring an "insult" aimed at the president to be a criminal offense.

The largest media channels are state operated, therefore the majority of respondents said they have access to state-run media rather than to private news. However, the Angolan national television, radio, and newspapers transmit little criticism of government officials. In addition, apart from coverage of reports on statements in the national assembly or during meetings with government officials, they do not give positive coverage of opposition parties and civil society activities (Unattributed interview 2004, 2005).

The concentration of media ownership in the hands of the government led to a narrowing of the range of voices and opinions being expressed in the mass media. The Angolan private media do not have the capacity to reach the widespread Angolan population. The TPA is the only television station that broadcasts from Luanda and most provincial capitals. Although satellite television is available, most Angolan citizens cannot afford it.

There are five province-based commercial radio stations and six privately owned weekly newspapers that have openly criticized government policies. However, their echoes with the Angolan population remain insignificant. Only 44 percent of the respondents on average followed the news from private radios, but about 21 percent never even had access to private news. This is because the Angolan government allowed private radio stations to broadcast only within their respective provinces, including the Catholic Church's Radio Ecclesia and Radio Lac Luanda (Unattributed interview 2004). Hence, in provinces where there are no private radio stations, people have no other alternative than to follow information from state-owned channels.

The private newspapers in Angola pay increased attention to issues such as the electoral process, corruption, governance, social conditions, and human rights. However, their scarcity and cost make them ineffective in passing independent news to the majority of Angolan people. The six private newspapers only print up to 25,000 copies per week (R. Marques 2006). Hence, only one in 20,000 Angolans has a chance to buy a copy of a private weekly newspaper. Compared to *Jornal de Angola* (JA), which costs roughly $ 0.50, the average price of one copy of the private newspaper is about $3, and that makes it difficult for the majority of poor people to purchase one.

Moreover, sometimes government authorities confiscate indepen-dent publications, and the state-owned airline (TAG) refuses to carry private media publications into provinces. The government has tolerated some criticisms of its policies and actions in the independent media; however, defamation of the president or his representatives is a crime punishable by imprisonment or fine (Bureau of Democracy, Human Rights, and Labor 2007). In addition, high-ranking government officials have pressured independent media to portray the government in a more favorable light. The government-owned media has frequently criticized independent journalists and opposition leaders.

It is obvious that despite the Angolan constitution stipulating the right to freedom of expression and even though Angola has ratified binding international treaties related to freedom of expression, the government is doing little to promote and protect it. Although the right to freedom of expression is not absolute, as it is placed within a context of competing values, its promotion can allow Angolan people to have a say on issues affecting their living conditions. Most importantly, it gives them the ability to hold their government accountable through a system of checks and balances of power. Therefore, unlawful limitations of freedom of expression can contribute to the deterioration of democratic governance and sustainable human development in post-conflict Angola.

2.1.2. Freedom of Association

Freedom of association is the right for people to come together and collectively express and defend common interests. The right to freedom of association has been included in a number of national constitutions and human rights instruments. The respect for the freedom of association by all public authorities and the exercising of this freedom by all sections of society are essential both to establish a democratic governance and to ensure that, once achieved, it remains healthy and flourishing (Smith 2005). In this regard, the formation of political parties is a significant manifestation of the freedom of association. However, freedom of association includes a vast array of interests, such as culture, recreation, sport, and social and humanitarian assistance.

The Angolan constitution and law provide for the right of association, which includes the right for citizens to form or belong to socio-political organizations of their choice. However, as discussed earlier with regards to the right to political participation or demonstration, the majority of respondents accused the Angolan government of making it difficult for Angolan people to enjoy their freedom of association (see Table 2.2).

Table 2.2 Issues over Freedom of Association*
Origin Crosstabulation

Questions/Response categories		Respondents			Total
		Coastal	Countryside	Expatriate	
Is there freedom to establish an organization (political party or NGO)	Easily	8	5	-	13
	Not easily	42	38	16	96
	Not at all	4	3	-	7
	Total	54	46	16	116
Are people free to join or belong to any political party?	Yes	8	9	4	21
	No	46	37	12	95
	Total	54	46	16	116
Is there sufficient public funding for opposition parties?	Yes	5	3	-	8
	No	33	28	4	65
	N/A	16	15	12	43
	Total	54	46	16	116
Does the MPLA government authorise demonstrations?	Easily	4	2	-	6
	Not easily	50	44	16	110
	Total	54	46	16	116
Is there unreasonable government interference in the internal affairs of opposition parties and NGOs	Often	39	32	16	87
	Not often	7	6	-	13
	Not at all	8	8	-	16
	Total	54	46	16	116

Questions/Response categories		Respondents			Total
		Coastal	Countryside	Expatriate	
Is the government doing enough to promote your freedom of Association?	Yes	8	4	-	12
	No	44	38	15	97
	N/A	2	4	1	7
	Total	54	46	16	116

Freedom of association is regulated by specific legislation that defines an association and establishes requirements for legal recognition (Lei no 14/91 1991). Associations are required to apply for registration and founding statute to the Ministry of Justice. If the ministry is satisfied with the documentation, it will publish the association's statute in the official government gazette, *Diário da República*. After this publication, the association sends a copy of the Diário da República to the attorney general (Procurador Geral da República) to register the association's statute. The association should then be sent an official registration number, proof of its registration as a legally recognized entity.

As in the case of freedom of expression, women's right to freedom of association is not well promoted, as women organizations are still very weak in Angola. Like other members of the civil society in Angola, women organizations lack capacity, influence, and coordination. The majority of women's organizations are vague in their role and objectives, reflecting a more general weakness in Angolan civil society, with the result that they have had little influence on policies that could improve women's lives.

The weakness of women's organizations was mainly because the war has had differing effects on women. The social reality of poor women, whether in rural or urban areas, differs greatly from that of more privileged women.[41] Moreover, critics argue that the reason women's organizations are failing to represent the interests of women at grassroots level is the fact that their leadership is often in the hands of privileged women who have separate agendas due to their strong links with political parties (Ducados 2004). For example, the OMA, which is Angola's largest women's organization, is also a political wing of the MPLA. OMA's political connection to the ruling party prevents many Angolan women from joining, and its leadership would find it difficult to defend the interests of all Angolan women.

Although the government issued a new presidential decree to regulate activities of non-governmental organization (NGOs) in Angola, the requirements for registration have not been amended. As authorization is required for a political party or civil society organizations to be formed, the Angolan government is accused of sometimes deliberately rejecting registrations from NGOs on the pretext of security grounds. An NGO leader in Luanda said that "although the Angolan government recognizes the right for NGOs and political parties to form, the Ministry of Justice continues to refuse registration to local human rights organizations" (Unattributed interview 2004, 2005). For example, Amnesty International has condemned the arbitrary ban of Mpalabanda (Associação Cívica de Cabinda), the only human rights organization operating in the province of Cabinda (Amnesty International 2006).

It is important to point out that some members of opposition parties and civil society manifest the right to freedom of association in a bad way. Since the introduction of multiparty politics in 1991, there has been a proliferation of political parties and civil society organizations. Most of these parties and NGOs remained one-person shows predominantly based in Luanda (BTI 2007). Only a few appear to be strong and have the necessary capacity to represent people's needs and voices. In 2007, there were about 360 NGOs registered with the Non-Governmental Forum in Angola (Forum das Organizações Não Governamentais de Angola—FONGA). However, most of these NGOs exist only on paper, and a genuine assessment of those still surviving and implementing projects needs to be conducted (BTI 2007).

One of the ruling party's MPs has said that the majority of opposition parties and civil society do not have a clear vision. He said "democratization means more than just having hundreds of political parties and NGOs" (Unattributed interview 2004). This criticism was shared by many ordinary people in Angola. For example, a group of students at Agostinho Neto University in Luanda said that many micro-parties have been formed not to represent the views of people but to create a kind of cent seeking—a source of revenue for their leaders. These parties are what Paguntke describes as parties without firm social roots, as they do not have connections with the people (Paguntke 2002).

In fact, the legislature has already set up regulations and legal restrictions to avoid proliferation of non-genuine parties. For example, the Angolan law of political parties enacted in 2005 would make it difficult for parties that do not have members to form or exist (Lei no 2/05 2005). Article 14 states that in order for a political party to be registered it must have a minimum 7,500 members, of which approximately 150 must reside in each of the Angolan provinces. The regulation in the new law may help to diminish the number of minor parties and leave the field for effective parties. However, critics argue that despite the amendment, the threshold of entry is still pretty low.

The Angolan government has been constantly accused of using unconstitutional methods to prevent electoral opposition parties to function properly. The government has continuously intimidated leaders of civil society and opposition parties in order to weaken their organization (Unattributed interview 2004). For example, in March 2007, allegations were made by UNITA that police tried to assassinate its leader, Isaias Samakuva (IRIN 2007). The incident caused concern about the political climate in the run-up to the 2008 legislative elections in Angola. The restrictions and intimidations imposed on political parties mainly outside Luanda had a negative effect on the electoral campaign that further undermined the process of building genuine democratic institutions in Angola

The Angolan constitution and binding international treaty ratified by Angola stipulate that everyone has the right to freedom of peaceful assembly and to freedom of association at all levels, in particular, in political, trade union, and civic matters, which means the right of everyone to form and to join trade unions for the protection of their interests. However, evidence shows that the right to freedom of association is far from protected. Failure to promote and protect freedom of association has had negative implications on the attempt to build democratic institutions for sustainable human development in post-conflict reconstruction of Angola.

2.1.3. Freedom of Movement

In addition to freedoms of expression and association, freedom of movement can enable citizens to enjoy their well-being. Among others, freedom of movement includes the right to leave and to return to one's own country, as well as the right to circulate within the country. Legal regulations to freedom of movement vary from one country to another. However, several international agreements beyond those prescribed by the United Nations govern freedom of movement within the African continent. The African Charter on Human and People's Rights, Article 12, guarantees that every individual has the right to freedom of movement within the borders of their own country as long as they abide by the state's laws. With free movement, people are safe to circulate and freely choose their residence. Civil society organizations can easily organize their mission trips across the country. More importantly, freedom of movement presents a great opportunity for political parties to reach people and spread their programs.

During the fieldwork in Angola, as Table 2.3 shows, research participants were asked strategic questions in order to ascertain the nature of freedom of movement in the post-civil era. The general findings show that the major challenges to freedom of movement in Angola are poor infrastructure, landmines, and street insecurity (mainly in Luanda). Women's freedom of movement is not restricted per se, but limited due to insecurity.

Table 2.3 Issues related to Freedom of Movement* Origin Crosstabulation

Questions/Response categories		Respondents			Total
		Coastal	Countryside	Expatriate	
Are you free to travel across the county?	**Yes**	7	13	-	20
	No	47	33	16	96
	Total	54	46	16	116
What makes it difficult for you to travel across the country?	**Poor infrastructures**	51	39	16	106
	Fear of persecution	3	7	-	10
	Total	54	46	16	116

Questions/Response categories		Respondents			Total
		Coastal	**Countryside**	**Expatriate**	
What is the great-est fear you have while moving from one place to another?	**Police Harass-ment**	**11**	-	-	11
	Robbery	**43**	-	**16**	59
	Anti personal mines	-	**46**	-	46
	Total	54	46	16	116

About 91 percent of respondents said that poor transport infrastructure is severely hampering freedom of movement in Angola. The twenty-seven-year-long civil war in Angola left the country's transport infrastructure in a dreadful state. Broken bridges and poor roads prevent people from moving easily from one place to another. Roads and railways, mainly in the countryside, were largely destroyed and neglected. Air travel was mostly used during the war because of military insecurity in the countryside. Angola has thirteen airports, all of which are in need of renovation. The road network is even less developed in the eastern and northern parts of the country. In villages without roads, the average distance to the nearest road is five kilometers—public transportation is available to only half of the communities (AFDB/OECD 2007). Accordingly, rebuilding the transport infrastructures should be considered a top priority in post-conflict Angola.

The Angolan government has been actively involved in the rehabilitation of primary transport infrastructure. For example, the state's 2006 draft budget gave high priority to transport infrastructure, with allocations increasing by 10 percent in real terms to reach 10 percent of total outlay (AFDB/OECD 2007). The government attested that it would use the 2.25 billion Chinese bilateral loans in the rehabilitation of dams, roads, and bridges that would improve the movement of people and goods (IRIN 2007).

However, the outcome of the government's efforts to rehabilitate primary transport infrastructure is still insufficient. Lack of well-structured public transport is another impediment to people's enjoyment of their freedom of movement. Transport is a nightmare in Luanda, which is home of more than one-third of the Angolan population. The so-called "Engarrafamento" (traffic jam) causes huge stress to the inhabitants of Luanda, which has negative effects on their well-being. Fewer highways and a shortage of parking spaces are among the major causes of Engarrafamento in Luanda, which prevents the people's enjoyment of freedom of movement.

People in Luanda spend hours waiting for taxis or the even more infrequent public buses. The state-run urban road transport company (TCUL) and other private public transportation companies, such as MACOM, are far from meeting the basic need of movement of people in Luanda. The so-called "Candongueiro," the private menu-buses (described as taxis in Angola), that facilitate the circulation of the majority of people in Luanda are often in bad condition.

Passenger seats in these Candongueiro are generally modified, unsecured, which presents less chance of survival in case of accidents. Transport fares for Candongueiro change on a daily basis, presenting a dilemma to travelers. The uncertainty of daily transport fares causes a headache mainly to students, whose budgets are often very limited. As a result, some students have no choice but to walk kilometers on end and to spend much longer in order to reach their schools, colleges, universities, or homes. The new Angolan transport legislation sets out useful regulations to tackle issues of road safety and to pay particular attention to Candongueiro. Nonetheless, the dilemma of transportation of persons in cities, mainly in Luanda, will be attenuated only if the country's urban transport system is reorganized. There is a need for more means of public transport (buses, train), roads, parking, and so on.

Another major obstacle to freedom of movement in Angola is the widespread possession of small guns by civilians. Following the 2002 cease-fire, there has been proliferation of small arms that cause major insecurity in the life of many Angolan people. There is no clear and exact number of how many guns are either in active use or stockpiled by ordinary citizens. In 2006, the estimated number of weapons in Angola ranged from 1.5 to 4 million (IRIN 2006). The circulation and availability of small arms in the hands of civilians has largely contributed to the increase in crimes and robberies in Luanda. Therefore, an effective and full-scale disarmament of civilians is urgently needed.

There are extensive empirical studies of the disarmament, demobilization, and reinsertion of former combatants (DDR) but less has been written about the disarmament of civilians. During the war, both the MPLA and UNITA distributed large numbers of small arms to civilians. In addition, as military service in Angola is compulsory, the majority of Angolan men over twenty-five were once sent to the frontline; therefore, some are likely to keep a weapon at home. The Angolan Interior Ministry has already launched a campaign for disarmament of civilians. The campaign is facing major challenges as some civilians are still hesitant to give up their weapons (IRIN 2006).

The disarmament of civilians is bound to fail if the government does not address basic social problems. Two main observations can be drawn as to why so many civilians in Angola are refusing to disarm (IRIN 2006). First, the increase in crime rates in places like Luanda and the inability of the national police force to tackle crime encourage people to buy or keep their weapons for self-defense (Unattributed interview 2005).

Second, unemployment and general life uncertainty constrain some civilians to keep their weapons. This category of civilians is more likely to commit gun crimes and robberies. After extensive conversations with some ordinary people in Luanda, someone said that a situation of complete despair leads some civilians in Angola to commit crimes. For example, Alberto,[42] a twenty-nine-year-old former combatant of the Angolan army said that he was forced to join the army when he was sixteen. He did not go to school, and he has been a reserve soldier since the end of war. He said, "Now the peace has come, I no longer have a salary; I do not have any idea how to feed my wife and three kids. . . . What can I do? I have a gun, it is the only bread I have—I would prefer to die in the streets with my guns than dying of hunger at home."

The Alberto's situation is similar to that of many other former combatants. The DDR program in Angola has paid much more attention to former UNITA combatants. In order to decrease crime rates in the streets, which jeopardize the fundamental freedom of movement and others' fundamental rights, the disarmament process should include former combatants from both sides as well as civilians (Knight and Ozerdem 2004).

The protection and abuse of freedom of movement within national and international borders can have a deep effect upon other basic human rights outlined in the Universal Declaration of Human Rights and other treaties. Denied the right to leave one's home, an individual may be politically repressed, prevented from practicing her/his chosen religion, prevented from enjoying the basic right to health, work, or education that ultimately could enhance her/his quality of life. Thus, while free movement may seem on the surface to be a fairly minor and obvious human right, it is in fact one of the most basic rights that in many countries around the world, when violated, causes numerous problems and instances of suffering. This is why limited enjoyment of freedom of movement contributes to the difficulties of sustainable human development in post-conflict Angola.

Promoting and protecting fundamental freedoms of association, expression, and movement is essential for the post-conflict reconstruction. These freedoms are at the core of the process of building democratic institutions in Angola, as they have an instrumental role in giving people a voice and a constructive role in shaping values and norms. The Angolan Government must open up and allow its people to enjoy their fundamental freedoms, which are crucial in inducing social responses to economic needs, as well as vital to the conceptualization of economic needs.

2.2. Economic, Social, and Cultural Rights

This section analyses the nature of rights to health, education, and work after the Luena Memorandum of understanding. The three rights correlate with the indicators used in the UNDP's Human Development Index (HDI).[43] Economic, social, and cultural rights relate to the conditions necessary to meet basic human needs such as food, water, housing, education, health care, and employment.

These rights are found in the International Covenant on Economic, Social, and Cultural Rights (ICESCR). The ICESCR is considered the International Bill of Human Rights, along with the Universal Declaration of Human Rights (UDHR) and the International Covenant on Civil and Political Rights (ICCPR), including the latter's first and second optional protocols. Among regional human rights instruments, the African Charter on Human and Peoples' Rights is considered to place the most emphasis on economic, social, and cultural rights. Moreover, socioeconomic and cultural rights are incorporated in the Committee on the Elimination of Discrimination Against Women[44] (CEDAW).

2.2.1. Right to Health

The right to health is indispensable for the exercise of other human rights and for a better life. Everybody is entitled to the enjoyment of the highest attainable standard of health conducive to living a life in dignity. The realization of the right to health may be pursued through numerous complementary approaches, such as the formulation of health policies, the implementation of health programs developed by the World Health Organization (WHO), and the adoption of specific legal instruments (CESCR 2000). The right to health includes certain components that are legally enforceable.

Under international human rights standards, member states have a duty to protect and promote the right to health. With reference to the existing empirical data on health condition in Angola and as shown in Table 2.4, it can be observed that the major social indicators of the right to health, such as life expectancy, malnutrition, housing, and access to water and sanitation deteriorated generally during the war and are still alarming (WHO 2005, 2006; BTI 2007).

Table 2.4 Issues related to Right to Health* Origin Crosstabulation

Questions/Response categories		Respondents			Total
		Coastal	Countryside	Expatriate	
What is the housing situation in Angola?	Good	8	-	-	8
	Bad	44	19	16	79
	N/A	2	27	-	29
	Total	54	46	16	116
Is food available in the markets?	Yes	46	-	9	55
	No	-	46	7	53
	N/A	8	-	-	8
	Total	54	46	16	116
How good is the supply of electrical power?	Good	-	12	-	12
	Bad	48	4	16	68
	N/A	6	30	-	36
	Total	54	46	16	116

Questions/Response categories		Respondents			Total
		Coastal	Countryside	Expatriate	
Do people have access to clean water?	Easily	11	-	-	11
	Not easily	43	35	16	70
	N/A	-	11	-	35
	Total	54	46	16	116
Are people able to access hospitals or other medical centres?	Easily	10	1	-	11
	Not easily	44	32	16	92
	N/A	-	13	-	13
	Total	54	46	16	116
What is the quality of medical staff and instruments?	Good	7	4	2	13
	Average	25	11	5	41
	Bad	22	31	9	62
	Total	54	46	16	116
Is it easy to find appropriate medical drugs in hospitals?	Easily	9	-	-	9
	Not easily	32	17	16	65
	Not at all	13	29	-	42
	Total	54	46	16	116

In order to reassess the general views of people on health condition in Angola, the fieldwork questionnaire on the right to health consisted of two categories. The first category looks at key factors related to healthcare in Angola. It analyses three variables: the availability, accessibility, and quality of health care. As shown in Table 2.4, only a few respondents said that people could easily access healthcare. There are two reasons to explain this finding: the first one is the shortage of hospitals or health posts, and the second reason is the fact that the cost of healthcare is high.

The heavy cost of civil war meant that insignificant resources were allocated to the health system over more than two decades, thus causing a shortage of hospitals or health centers, mainly in the interior of Angola. According to the WHO's 2006 report, massive medical infrastructures, about 65 percent of health units were destroyed during the war. Despite the fact that public expenditure on health is relatively high, health indicators in Angola are extremely poor. Therefore, a critical study should be made in order to explore who is benefiting from the health budgets and what the scope for a more efficient and more equitable spending on health in Angola is.

According to existing secondary data, Angola is one of the countries in the world with the lowest life expectancy: thirty-nine years for men and forty-one years for women. "Infant and under-five mortality rates, estimated at 195 and 265 per 1,000 live births per year respectively, are among the world's highest. Malaria, acute respiratory and diarrheal disease, tetanus and malnutrition, combined with poor access to healthcare, damaged the infrastructure and the lack of trained health professionals, are the main causes of mortality" (WHO 2005). According to the United Nations Children's Fund (UNICEF 2006), Angola has one of the highest under-five mortality rates in the world. Malnutrition is an important underlying condition, estimated to affect almost half of Angola's 7.4 million children (AFDB/OECD 2007).

Women in particular have seen their human right to health deteriorate both during and after the civil war. The long period of war in Angola has impoverished the majority of the Angolan population, and women were the worst affected. Searching for survival, some young women turned to prostitution, which exposed some of them to sexually transmitted diseases and they have serious health problems. After the 2002 cease-fire, the government launched a large demobilization, disarmament and reintegration program. However, non-combatant women were excluded from any direct benefit as the program covered only a set number of UNITA and Angolan Armed Forces (FAA) soldiers and did not make specific provisions for vulnerable groups like widows and UNITA wives (Ducados 2004).

In 2000, the United Nations Committee on Economic, Social, and Cultural Rights, the Covenant's supervisory body, adopted a General Comment on the right to health that provides a normative interpretation of the right to health as enshrined in Article 12 of the

Covenant. This General Comment interprets the right to health as an inclusive right that extends not only to timely and appropriate health care but also to those factors that determine good health . Accordingly, the second category of the right to health questionnaire assesses five major factors related to public health in Angola.

The first major factor is food, which is one of the crucial components of the right to health. Everyone has a fundamental right to be free from hunger and malnutrition. In 2004, the member states of the World Food Organization (FAO) unanimously adopted the right to food Guidelines, which are a practical tool to assist countries in their efforts to eradicate hunger (FAO 2005). The guidelines are a set of rational recommendations on, among others, labor, land, water, genetic resources, sustainability, safety nets and education (WHO 2003). They also encourage the allocation of budgetary resources to anti-hunger and poverty programs. By recognizing the Right to Food, governments have an obligation to respect, protect, and fulfill this right.

As shown in Table 2.4, while the majority of respondents from the coastal region said that a supply of food actually exists (though very expensive); those living in the countryside stated that there is a scarcity of food. Unlike the colonial era, Angola is much more dependent on food from abroad. Due to the state of war during that period, the imported food was circulating mainly in the coastal region, namely in Luanda. However, despite the fact that food was available, there was not enough for everyone. As a result, critics have argued that suppliers had an opportunity to implement 'market power,[45] or monopoly as they had the ability to change the market price. This monopoly greatly benefits the minority rich people, thus leaving the majority poor Angolan in despair.

Despite the end of civil war in 2002, supermarkets are still enjoying their monopoly. For example Luanda, a city of over four million inhabitants has roughly 15 supermarkets (Fieldwork notes 2005). The price of goods in these supermarkets is extremely high and only affordable for the minority of middle and upper class of the population. The majority of the population goes to the informal market where the hygiene conditions are very poor (Tonet 2005).

In the countryside region the situation was even worse where during the twenty-seven years of civil war thousands of people died from hunger (MSF 2002). To some extent, widespread famine in the countryside was caused by the deliberate strategies of war.[46] The situation in the countryside of Angola remains critical despite the end of the war. There is still a widespread food shortage. The lack of transport infrastructure, in some provinces, makes it difficult to transport imported food from the coastal region to the countryside. Despite the fact that agricultural production in countryside is beginning to recover,[47] the FAO is alarmed that the rise in production is smaller than the country estimation. As a result, the country has to import three-quarters of its food requirements (AFDB/OECD 2007). The shortage of food, quantitatively and qualitatively, has a negative effect on post-war reconstruction in Angola.

The second major factor of public health analysis is the right to water. Like food, water is essential to sustain life. In 2002, the United Nations Committee for the International Covenant on Economic, Social, and Cultural Rights adopted water as a human right. The rights is protected in the right to life and dignity, as set forth in the international human rights instruments (Langford 2000). Drawing on a range of international treaties and declarations, it stated that "the right to water clearly falls within the category of guarantees essential for securing an adequate standard of living, particularly since it is one of the most fundamental conditions for survival"(WHO 2003).

The right to water can be desecrated through many forms, including industrial pollution of water sources, failure to provide purification and sanitation for the urban poor, and pricing of water delivery beyond the reach of the rural poor. It should be noted that although there is sufficient water for every person's basic needs in all eighteen provinces of Angola, access to clean water is extremely difficult. This is because there is not sufficient infrastructure to carry water to locations inside or close to households, or for communities to gain access to ground water (Redvers 2008). The majority of people in the countryside usually collect water from rivers and use it without any purification. Perhaps, therefore, most of the respondents from the countryside were indifferent to the question of clean water, as they do not have others alternatives. Using water from rivers without purification can provoke fatal diseases. However, due to lack of public education, people remain ignorant and continue to consume dirty water (Redvers 2008).

In the towns in the coastal region, there is some water infrastructure; however, the main challenge is the distribution, as well as the existing supply network, and facilities in cities do not ensure that water is of an adequate quality. According to the WHO statistics, the proportion of people with piped water in the whole of Angola is 33 percent (WHO 2006). For example, in Luanda tap water exists only in the city center, and water is regular in rich residential places and in ministerial and diplomatic offices. The majority of ordinary people in Luanda buys water from lorries and keeps it in their domestic reservoirs for weeks.[48]

The monthly cost of water for citizens who buy water from lorries is much higher than the bills for tap water. Furthermore, the conservation of water for long periods in domestic reservoirs may result in problems of sanitation. Hence, there is the high risk that people pick up diseases related to dirty water. For example, Angola's worst cholera epidemic in 2006 was largely due to overcrowding, a shortage of clean water, and poor sanitation (UNICEF 2006). Deprived urban and rural areas are totally ignored in infrastructure development and maintenance. Also, they do not receive assistance with small-scale water purification technologies. Therefore, the lack of clean drinking water further contributes to the poor living conditions of Angolan people.

The third major factor of public health analyzed was sanitation and hygiene. Despite the fact that sanitation has often been neglected, its critical role in preserving life is also increasingly recognized. At the world summit on sustainable development in 2002, the international community pledged to halve the percentage of people without access to basic sanitation by 2015. This pledge complements the Millennium Declaration's commitment to reduce by half the proportion of people unable to reach or afford safe drinking water. However, Angola has been criticized for not doing enough to improve the sanitation condition and hygiene, mostly in the country's main city Luanda (WHO 2007).

There are public and private initiatives to make the city of Luanda clean, but the impact is still small. Although the interior of Angola is more undeveloped, it is relatively cleaner than Luanda, the capital city and the most populated city of Angola. The absence of adequate sanitation systems in Angola, mainly in Luanda, leads to widespread pollution of water sources that communities rely upon for survival. In addition, the presence of fecal contaminants in water is one of the leading causes of diarrhea in Angola. For example, poor sanitation was one of the main causes of the 2006 outbreak of cholera in Angola, which produced over 70,000 cases and claimed the lives of nearly 3,000 people (IRIN 2007). Thus, poor sanitation has a direct connection to the deprived living conditions of people in Angola.

Housing was the fourth major factor of public health analyzed. Decades of war and lack of appropriate economic and legal reforms have posed a serious housing problem in Angola. Of the 37 percent of the Angolan population that is urban, 90 percent live in settlements without a clearly defined legal status (UNFPA 2007). Some live in multi-family houses that were constructed in the 1960s and have since deteriorated to the point that basic utilities are limited or unavailable (AFDB/OECD 2007).

Adequate housing is crucial for the enjoyment of human dignity and health. Without a right to housing, many other basic rights will be compromised, including the right to privacy and the right to assembly and association. The right to housing is clearly recognized in international law. Article 25 of the UDHR provides, "Everyone has the right to a standard of living adequate for the health and well-being of himself and his family, including . . . housing."[49] Further recognition of the right to housing can be found in many other international treaties.[50]

Angola's response to the right to housing has been a mixed one to date. On the positive side, the right to housing is recognized and supported in the Angolan National Constitution in Article 25. However, there remains considerable room for improvement, especially in relation to particular groups of Angolans. Housing is a very serious problem in Angola, mainly in Luanda. As a result of rapid urbanization, immense informal settlements, the so-called "Musseque" (slums) have emerged in urban areas. The rapid expansion of new neighborhoods and the spread of slums have stressed the urban water supply and sanitation systems. The lack of these basic services poses serious hygiene and health problems. There is a complete absence of maintenance of many houses and buildings in Angola. The price of real estate is very high, and most people cannot afford to pay for a mortgage. In addition, landlords in some areas ask tenants to pay several months of rent in advance in US dollars.

One of the remarkable aspects of housing in post-conflict Angola is the building skyscrapers in Luanda. In addition, a brand new zone (Talatona), composed of compounds with leisure houses, has been built in Luanda. But critics argue that the construction of these skyscrapers and Talatona is one of "white elephant" projects that targets the minority rich people or aims to show off but does not satisfy the majority of Angolan people. The large majority of Angola continues to live in musseque. They cannot afford either to buy or rent an apartment/house in the Talatona or in the new skyscrapers.

Hundreds of thousands of returning refugees, internally displaced persons, and former combatants face frightening challenges in reintegrating into Angolan society. "Families return to devastated communities and settle on land that is heavily covered with anti-personal mines (Takirambudde 2007). The elderly, disabled persons, widows, and female heads of households experience the worst situations, mainly in rural areas (HRW 2005). According to the Angola's National Agency for Private Investment (ANIP), the city of Luanda was built to sustain a population of 700,000 and now it is the home of around 4 million people (ANIP 2007).

Accordingly, construction or rehabilitation of adequate housing should be considered one of the highest priorities of the government's agenda in post-conflict Angola as a way to consolidate efforts of sustaining human development. Urbanization of Angola will necessitate some kind of sacrifices. While some musseques in Luanda will require renovation, others will need to be completely demolished in order build new houses. However, to avoid critics like those in 2006 when houses in the musseque of "Boa-Vista" were destroyed,[51] the demolishing of ghettoes should be preceded by a systematic planning for relocation of the population and compensations if required.

The Angolan government housing policy in post-conflict Angola is of mixed perspectives: On one hand, since 2002, the government has made some effort to sponsor housing construction projects. On the other hand, Angola still have a long way to go in order to develop a housing system afford by the majority of its poor people. On April 13, 2008, during his opening speech for the National Conference on Urban Development and Housing, the Angolan President, Eduardo dos Santos, attested the fact that to own a house is a challenge that we need to overcome. As a result, the president declared that the Angolan government is going to build one million houses within the next four years. The idea of building new houses is welcome by all Angola. However, it is still unclear what quality these houses will be—how affordable will they be and what will be the quota for each of the provinces? Now four years later, despite several statements by

President dos Santos of a commitment to assure adequate housing for all Angolans, housing conditions are still precarious, a large proportion of the population lacks proper accommodation as well as forced evictions continue.

The fifth major factor of public health analyzed was the right to electricity. People's right to electricity is incorporated into international human rights standards. Article 11(1) of the ICESCR stipulates that everyone has a right to "an adequate standard of living . . . including . . . housing, and to the continuous improvement of living conditions." Access to electricity has been incorporated into the human right to adequate housing. The UN member stated that the 2002 World Summit on Sustainable Development (WSSD) in Johannesburg undertook "to improve access to reliable and affordable energy services for sustainable development sufficient to facilitate the achievement of the MDGs" (UN 2002; UN Fact Sheet 2002). Hence, considering electricity as an essential civic service implies that governments should provide access to an equal supply of electricity to all individuals within their jurisdiction or control.

The 2006 International Energy Agency's report gave a rational update on Angola's current energy situation and identified the main priorities that could form the basis of an effective overall energy strategy (IEA 2006). Major portions of the power generation and transmission systems in Angola were seriously damaged during the civil war. However, despite the end of the war, the country was finding it difficult to rehabilitate energy infrastructure. According to ANIP, only about 15 percent of Angolan people have access to electric power (2007). This is why, as shown in Table 2.4, more than 50 percent of respondents stated that the condition of the energy infrastructure in Angola was not good. Moreover, most people in the countryside use firewood and oil light for their domestic energy; therefore, the majority of people there remain indifferent to the subject of the use of electric energy.

In the coastal region, mainly in Luanda, people are desperately in need of electricity and gas for domestic utilities. The distribution of gas in Luanda is less problematical than that of electricity. Energy infrastructure has not kept pace with the dynamism of the economy, especially in Luanda. The frequency of blackouts and power cuts has increased, due to inefficiencies in thermal generation facilities and delays in completing the construction of dams and hydroelectric plants (AFDB/OECD 2007). The electric service in Luanda is defective, and due to frequent power outages, many residences and businesses have generators (AFDB/OECD 2007). As the power outage duration is often undetermined, households rely much more on electricity produced by diesel generators than hydroelectric supply. The extensive use of power diesel generators in Angola mainly in Luanda creates huge air pollution, which has negative consequences on environment and well-being of people.[52]

To sum up, it can be argued that despite the fact that Article 47(1) of the Angolan constitution stipulates that "the state shall promote the measures needed to ensure the right of citizens to medical and health care" the majority of Angolan people are finding it difficult to enjoy this right. The poor conditions of the right to health contribute to the deterioration of living conditions in post-conflict Angola. The country needs to rationally use part of its national revenues to boost the health system. A healthier population is capable of sustaining economic growth and human development.

2.2.2. Right to Work

The right to work is crucial in the process of sustaining human development. It is preserved in the Universal Declaration of Human Rights and recognized in international human rights law through its inclusion in the International Covenant on Economic, Social, and Cultural Rights, where the right to work emphasizes economic, social, and cultural development. The right to work provides people with the opportunity to earn a living wage in a safe work environment and also gives people freedom to organize and bargain together. However, the right to work does not guarantee that every person will have a job; rather, it requests governments to take effective steps to realize the right over time. Governments breach the right to work when they either fail to take those steps or when they make the situation worse.

There are many aspects of the right to work that are particularly relevant to political rights and to equal citizenship. The right to work enables people to feel self-worth, gain self-confidence, and attain the necessary skills to exercise other rights. As such, "both liberal and democratic political theories are premised on the assumption that people are capable of self-determination: that they possess the capacity and confidence to take responsibility for their own lives, whether individually or collectively" (Beetham 2003). In order to understand the condition of right to work in Angola, the fieldwork's survey, as shown in Table 2.5, focused on three variables: availability of jobs, equal opportunity in employment, and the level of salary.

Table 2.5 Issues related to Right to Work*
Origin Crosstabulation

Questions/Response categories		Respondents			Total
		Coastal	Countryside	Expatriate	
Is it easy to find a job?	No	30	23	12	65
	Yes	17	15	-	32
	N/A	7	8	4	19
	Total	54	46	16	116
Are there equal opportunities for employment?	No	32	23	12	67
	Yes	15	15	-	30
	N/A	7	8	4	19
	Total	54	46	16	116
Is there gender equality in politics?	Yes	14	16	13	43
	No	39	28	-	67
	N/A	1	2	3	6
	Total	54	46	16	116
Is recruitment "politically manipulated?	Yes	37	27	12	76
	No	7	11	-	18
	N/A	10	8	4	22
	Total	54	46	16	116
Is recruitment racially, ethnically and regionally influenced?	Yes	37	26	12	75
	No	7	7	-	14
	N/A	10	13	4	27
	Total	54	46	16	116
Is the minimum wage in Angola adequate?	Enough	35	26	12	73
	Not enough	5	7	-	12
	N/A	14	13	4	31
	Total	54	46	16	116

There are two main things that contribute to the scarcity of jobs in Angola. First, there has been an extensive influx of people from the countryside to the coastal region, particularly in Luanda, as result of the civil war. The massive movement from the countryside has increased pressure on the urban infrastructure and the labor market. As most of the internally displaced persons (IDPs) were unskilled, they turned to the informal sector (Ammassari 2005). Despite the war being over, the majority of the migrants, mainly young people, do not want to return to the countryside, which they consider lacking in attractive living conditions. This situation contributes to the increased rate of unemployment and underemployment in bigger towns, as well as to the shortage of human resources in rural agriculture sectors—therefore, impeding the sustainability of human development.

The second reason for job scarcity in Angola is the slow investment in non-oil sectors. The government's new measures to deregulate economic activity, sustain the privatization process, and attract foreign investment in the non-oil sectors have been dawdling to produce results. The OECED' s 2007 report points out that private investors complain that risk-taking and job-creating activities in Angola is jeopardized by invalid regulations and rent-seeking behavior (AFDB/ OECD 2007). The Angolan business sector includes a small number of businesses considered to have strong political influence (the so-called *empresarios de confiança*—"trusted businesses"). There are many obstacles to entry for businesses that do not have these connections. The government has begun to address this issue through efforts to improve the tendering and auditing of public sector procurement contracts, among other things by employing new staff at the Accounts Tribunal (AFDB/OECD 2007).

Aguinaldo Jaime, the assistant minister to the former Prime Minister, said that the Angolan government was implementing a strategy of diversifying its economy, foreseeing a greater participation of the non-oil sector in the gross domestic product (IRIN 2007). The increase of the production in the non-mineral sector could indeed enable citizens to benefit directly from the Angolan economy's growth, since it is a field that creates most direct employment (Jaime 2007). However, members of civil society and opposition parties interviewed during the fieldwork were pessimistic about the government plan to diversify the economy and create more jobs.

Women, in particular, were overloaded with work as a result of civil war. They have taken many responsibilities usually performed by men, such as providing for the household, building and repairing houses, dealing with community leaders and government officials, and fulfilling religious and social obligations. Despite the end of the war, many women continue to perform these responsibilities, mainly because husbands have died or deserted the household. Women's earnings in the informal sector of the economy have started to pose a serious cultural challenge to men's income-earning abilities and to gender relations in the family. These changes may partly explain evidence of an upsurge in domestic violence against women and children since the early 1990s (Ducados 2004).

Finding suitable jobs has become more difficult even for the few skilled and qualified Angolans. Participants in my recent informal conversations in Luanda deplore the fact that it is much easier for foreigners to find work in Angola than Angolans. In many countries, including the majority of developed countries, priority for recruitment is given to national citizens.[53] In Angola, however, some companies and international organizations find it easy to violate the international labor standards and fill vacancies with international staff even where it was possible to find Angolans with more or less the same skills and qualifications. Moreover, expatriate workers in private companies and international organizations in Angola, regardless their experience and qualifications, receive proportionally higher salaries than their Angolan colleagues.[54] These practices of recruitment and treatment abuse the fundament right to work of Angolan people—therefore, there is need for a well-elaborated Angolan labor law to prevent such abuse.

Under international laws, discrimination in access to employment is strictly prohibited, including distinctions, exclusions, restrictions, or preferences, in law or practice, on the grounds of race, color, sex, political opinion, social origin, or age. In addition, the Angolan constitution also recognizes the right for non-discrimination in employment. However, despite Article 28(2) of the Angolan Constitution stipulating that "no citizens shall suffer discrimination in respect of employment," this regulation is routinely violated. This type of discrimination jeopardizes the attempt of building a qualified workforce for adequate post-conflict reconstruction of Angola.

Recruitment shall focus on merit and not on race or any group affiliation.

The third variable of the right to work studied is the quality of salary. Angola needs machinery for fixing, monitoring, and enforcing equitable minimum salaries that would be compatible to the cost-of-living index. Lower salaries and arrears in salary payments as well as poor working conditions act as major deterrents for Angolan jobseekers to enter the civil service (Ammassari 2005). The main cause of underpaid jobs in Angola is the lack of qualifications and the exodus of the population from rural to urban areas. Due to the scarcity of jobs, many Angolan people, mainly in Luanda, are ready to take underpaid positions. During the war, the majority of men were employed in military service. With the end of war, the Angolan Army had to cut its numbers, expanding the number of jobseekers.

Women who were abducted by UNITA soldiers face the impasse of whether or not to leave their UNITA husbands and return to their original villages, where they risk being rejected. In addition, the social reality of some UNITA supporters is critical for both men and women. Relationships with non-UNITA supporters remain difficult, with people still suspicious of each other and some reluctant to provide UNITA supporters with jobs (Fieldwork notes 2005).

The majority of former combatants were recruited when they were very young and did not have a chance to complete their studies. Accordingly, they do not have enough qualifications to compete in the post-conflict job-market. As a result, they are underemployed and receive poor salaries. For example, some former combatants work with private security companies. Ricardo, a former combatant, said that the net monthly salary of security guards varies from 150 to 350 US dollars. "It is difficult to live with so little money in Luanda," he said. "Therefore, if you see me walking and talking to you today, it is just by God's mercy," he added (Fieldwork notes 2004). This is true; one could argue that Luanda is one of the most expensive cities in the world.[55] Three hundred and fifty US dollars is almost nothing for monthly expenses.

The lack of better paid jobs in Angola forces some parents to abandon their responsibilities to their children, and this increases the rate of juvenile delinquency. For example, Ricardo is married and the father of four children. He said despite his wife selling goods in informal market, they cannot afford to send their children to school. His three children over ten years old are responsible for covering some of their basic needs, such as clothing. The case of Ricardo is not an isolated one; there are many underpaid employees in Angola who are finding it difficult to respond to their domestic responsibilities. Abandoned children are vulnerable to wave of delinquency, presenting further insecure environment in the society.

Despite the Angolan constitution in its Article 46 stipulating the right to work, there is still a lot to be done for availability of jobs, equal opportunity in employment, salary levels. The Angolan government should monitor companies (international and national) as well as international organizations and prohibit them from violating the fundamental right of work of Angolan people. Poor work conditions and salaries deny people's capability for self-determination. Moreover, a poor condition of right to work undermines prospect to sustain human development in the post-conflict Angola, as people do no longer possess the capacity and confidence to take responsibility for their lives.

2.2.3. Right to Education

The right to education is crucial in the process of sustaining human development. It is preserved in the Universal Declaration of Human Rights and recognized in international human rights law through its inclusion in the International Covenant on Economic, Social, and Cultural Rights—where the right to education emphasizes economic, social, and cultural development. As Beetham (2000) argues, education is a key economic and political right—one whose denial is especially damaging to the democratic principle of civil and political equality.

The right to education includes the right to free and compulsory primary education and increasing access to secondary, technical, vocational, and higher education. The right to education is necessary for the attainment of other basic economic and political rights; it provides the skills necessary to be an active citizen. It also increases their opportunities to realize other human rights, including the right to health and work. For example, without knowledge about nutrition or health care, the guarantee of basic sanitation will prove insufficient. Hence, failing to ensure people's right to education reduces their vulnerability to exploitation and many other human rights abuses.

Angolan people have never fully enjoyed their basic right to education. Under Portuguese rule, education was largely limited to the minority, as the colonial government declared the education of Africans to be "the exclusive responsibility of missionary personnel" (Collelo 1989). As a result, few Angolans had an opportunity to study during the colonial era. After independence, the Angolan government focused its efforts on basic education and literacy in areas it controlled. As a result, between 1976 and 1980, the number of students in the formal school system doubled, with over a million children enrolled in primary school and 105,000 in secondary school (Collelo 1991). However, the number of students enrolled decreased dramatically in 1980s due to the civil war. By 2001, there were still fewer students enrolled in primary school (approximately 1.6 million) than the 1.9 million children who were registered twenty years earlier (UNDP, et al. 2002). There were more students enrolled in school in 1980 than in the 2001.

The right to education is very crucial for sustaining human development in Angola. As James Elder argues, "Angola will recover when every boy and girl in every province is in school." According to Elder, 70 percent of the 13 million Angolan people are under the age of twenty-four; therefore, nurturing and educating the young people is absolutely critical to rebuilding a nation devastated by almost three decades of war (IRIN 2003). He argues that education would have significant influence on Angolan society, because apart from the obvious benefits, education gives children security and is a "stabilizing force in their lives" (IRIN 2003).

However, critics argue that the Angola commitment to the promotion of the right to education is very little. For example the former special rapporteur on the Right to Education, Katarina Tomasevski, stated that Angola may have one of the fastest growing African economies but its benefits are not trickling down to the population—the budget allocated to education is still insignificant (Tomasevski 2006). Hence, as shown in Table 2.6, the fieldwork survey on the right to education reassessed the following four variables: the availability of schools, colleges, and universities; the accessibility to education, the quality of education, and the salary of teachers and lecturers.

Table 2.6 Issues related to Right to Education* Origin Crosstabulation

Questions/Response categories		Respondents			Total
		Coastal	Countryside	Expatriate	
Are there enough infra-structures for education?	Yes	29	36	16	81
	No	25	-	-	25
	N/A	-	10	-	10
	Total	54	46	16	116
Is there equal opportunity of study in An-gola?	Yes	17	-	-	17
	No	29	39	16	84
	N/A	8	7	-	15
	Total	54	46	16	116
What is the quality of education in Angola?	Poor	29	35	16	80
	Average	10	11	-	21
	Good	15	-	-	15
	Total	54	46	16	116
Salary of teacher and lecturers	Not enough	17	14	-	31
	Enough and regular	32	24	10	66
	N/A	5	8	6	19
	Total	**54**	**46**	**16**	**166**

Based on findings represented in Table 2.6, it can be observed that there are three main obstacles to the enjoyment of the right to education in Angola. The first obstacle is the lack of schools, colleges, and other educational infrastructures. The twenty-seven years of civil war were the first cause of the lack of educational infrastructure in Angola. During the war, schools were destroyed—young boys were forced to join military services. The destruction of schools was exacerbated in rural areas where there was intense confrontation between the Angolan army and UNITA troops. This is why, perhaps, more than three quarter of respondents from the countryside said there are not enough infrastructures for education in the country.

Despite the war being over, building schools, colleges, or universities, mainly in the countryside region, will take time. According to a rural household survey conducted by OECD in 2005, the illiteracy rate among heads of household is 60 percent (AFDB/ OECD 2007). To address these challenges, the Ministry of Education has reformulated the plan for reconstruction of the education system (Plano-Quadro de Reconstrução do Sistema Educativo), setting new targets to be achieved by 2015 (IRIN 2003).

However, according to the United Nations Children's Fund (UNICEF)'s report, Angola is facing a big challenge of raising the number of children in primary school from an estimated 2.1 million in 2003 to 5 million by 2015 (UNICEF 2007). The 2003 Women's Commission for Refugee Women and Children[56] report on education in Angola found that while there are fewer girls than boys enrolled at each grade level, the differential between girls and boys does not increase throughout the primary and middle school years, which is common in many countries.

The second obstacle to the right to education is the fact that access to education is not open to all Angola people. Apart from shortage of infrastructure for education, high tuition fee in private schools, colleges, and universities is another obstacle to access to education in Angola. During the post-independence era, tuition fees were abolished. With its shift to the free market in the 1990s, Angola lost its commitment to free and compulsory education. Despite the fact that the constitution obliges the state to promote education, it does not assure either free or all-encompassing primary education. Although there is no legal guarantee of free education, the Angolan government is in favor of it. Studying at private schools, colleges, and universities is much more expensive than public educational institutions. However, most of respondents to questionnaire survey argue that the places in public institutions are limited and the quality of education is very poor compared to private institutions.

The third obstacle to the right of education in Angola is the poor quality of education in the country. About 60 percent of respondents said the quality of education in Angola is not good. The shortage of educational infrastructures and personnel as well as a widespread practice of corruption contributes to the poor quality of education in Angola. The long period of civil war in Angola had not only destroyed the infrastructures but it had impeded the rise of qualified human resources in all sectors, including education. As a result, schools, colleges, universities, and other vocational training centers have had to fill the gap with non- and under-qualified human resources (AFDB/OECD 2007).

Institutional and systemic strengthening of the education sector and related capacity building are a pre-requisite to take on this challenge. Some UN agencies such as United Nations Educational, Scientific, and Cultural Organization (UNESCO) and UNICEF are engaged in training primary school teachers in Angola (UNESCO 2004). However, both local and external observers argue that the Angolan government effort to promote the right to education is slow. Tomasevski argues that although poverty is often considered as the cause of exclusion from education in many parts of the world, the problem in Angola is wealth (Tomasevski 2006). The revenue generated from oil wealth could, to some extent, contribute to the quantitative and qualitative improvement in social conditions, including the educational sector. However, this is not the case as there is still little progress on health, work, and the education situation in the country.

Corruption and bribes jeopardize the quality of education. Hungry teachers are obliged to accept or ask for bribes, the so-called "gasosa" (soft drink), from students in exchange for good marks. This means some pupils do not prepare for their courses, as they are sure that they will give bribes to teachers and pass grades. During informal conversation with some teachers in Angola, most of them admitted that some of them accept bribes because they are often underpaid. The Angolan Ministry of Education has launched a campaign in the public mass media against bribes in schools. Arguing about this campaign, Zeca, a high school teacher said, "If they ask us to give up taking gasosa, we will then ask for cerveja (beer). Another teacher said that the best way to fight corruption in education is to increase salaries. "You cannot tell me to refuse gazoza while my children are dying from hunger," he said.

Despite Article 49 of the Angolan constitution stipulating that the state's obligation to promote access to education, this right has not been fulfilled adequately for decades. The poor condition of the right to education jeopardizes the prospect of sustainable human development in post-conflict Angola. Education would enable people to learn relevant skills and stand independently. For example, restoring transparency and public accountability during the electoral process requires informing citizens about the unacceptable risks of secret, privatized voting systems, and motivating them to demand transparency and public accountability from local election officials.

Moreover, the scarcity of human capital poses another major challenge to the promotion of rights to education in Angola. Despite some universities, such as Agostinho Neto, Universidade Catolica, and Jean-Piaget, recently agreeing to introduce master's degree programs in their curriculum, they do not have enough qualified lecturers to deliver post-graduate courses.[57] Therefore, to pursue post-graduate studies, most Angolan students go abroad.

However, studying abroad requires financial support, which the majority of Angolan students cannot afford. As a result, only a minority of Angolan students manage to pursue post-graduate degrees. Despite the fact that there are some foreign organizations supporting Angolans in pursuing their post-graduate studies abroad, these organizations are limited, and the scholarships are highly competitive.

The human right to education touches every aspect of human activity; therefore, studying and improving educational institutions are central to the prosperity and future of society. Education is both a human right in itself and an indispensable means of realizing other human rights. As an empowerment right, education is the primary vehicle by which economically and socially marginalized persons can lift themselves out of poverty and obtain the means to participate fully in their communities.

While promoting and protecting the right to education is crucial in reaching sustaining human development in the post-conflict Angola, decades of civil conflict, extremely limited access to countryside, inadequate funding for education, and poor human and resource capacity has created an education crisis. The government is short of schools and qualified teachers, and millions of students are outside the formal system, with limited access to either formal or non-formal opportunities. The situation is worse for IDPs and children in rural areas. Accordingly, since the majority of the population in Angola are still uneducated, it would be difficult for them to decide freely about their lifestyle and most importantly to participate efficiently in the post-conflict reconstruction of Angola. Therefore, in order to improve the living conditions for Angolans, major investments in education are highly encouraged.

Summary

The signing of the Luena Memorandum of Understanding on April 2002 brought a new era in Angola. It is for the first time ever in the post-independence era that Angola experienced more than nine years of a climate of peace. As a result, there is an opportunity to explore whether or not human development in post-conflict Angola is sustainable. The critical analysis of freedoms of expression, association, and movement as well as rights to health, education, and work has enabled me to assess people's living conditions in post-conflict Angola. The main finding is that the state of human development in Angola is not sustainable. Many Angolan citizens, particularly in the countryside, are still waiting to enjoy the benefits of peace dividends. Deprived socioeconomic conditions pose a great challenge to human development in post-conflict Angola. The promotion of fundamental human rights is crucial in the attempt to achieve sustainable human development.

The analysis of women rights was incorporated into the discussion of the six basic rights for human development. Although Angolan women play a major role in the promotion of human development, there is still widespread gender inequality in Angolan politics. The main cause of political gender discrimination is of a historical nature and can be attributed to structural organization of the two belligerent parties, MPLA and UNITA. The long period of war allowed men in high military and political positions in Angola. Although the two parties have women's wings, they had no influence in the decision-making process. Therefore, there is an urgent need to readjust gender relations to the needs of both women and men, as an essential component for sustainable development in post-conflict Angola.

The promotion of the six basic rights for human development requires both financial means and political willingness. For example, promoting the right to education involves aspects such as building public schools and training teachers, which requires public investment. The question is what can be done to transform Angola's potential wealth into real wealth that benefits the entire Angolan population. To answer this question, critical studies of the macroeconomic situation in Angola should be undertaken, in order to analyze the economic challenge and prospective for human development in post-conflict Angola.

III. POST-CONFLICT ANGOLA MACROECONOMIC SITUATION

The war and control of natural resources between belligerent parties was the major obstacle to human development in Angola. Even though the MPLA has managed to stay in power, it blamed the state of war for the poor economic performance prior to 2002. The government's attempt to promote economic growth was hindered on by the fact that UNITA controlled much of Angola, including its valuable diamond mines, and by the government's large military budget.

Although Angola is still recovering from almost three decades of civil war, its economy was the fastest growing in Africa for six consecutive years before 1999. However, the discussion in the preceding chapter shows that despite the end of war, people's living conditions in Angola have not improved. Therefore, in order to understand why Angola is finding it difficult to transform its economic growth into sustainable human development in post-conflict Angola, it is crucial to analyze the country's economic factors. This can enable us to understand the country's macroeconomic situation, policies, and how economic growth could affect human development in Angola.

Accordingly, this chapter analyses the macroeconomic situation in post-conflict Angola and its capacity to influence sustainable human development. The first section looks at the macroeconomic setting in post-conflict Angola. It examines both advantageous and challenging aspects to economic growth in post-conflict Angola. The second section analyses the correlation between economic growth and human development in Angola.

3.1. Angola's National Output

The analysis of national output is crucial in the attempt to examine the sources of national income and wealth Angola has available to promote human development in the post-conflict era. In order to have an approximate figure of Angolan national output, reference can be made to data published by international financial institutions in collaboration with the Angolan Ministry of Finance and the World Bank. Accordingly, the following Table 3.1 represents a selection of the key macroeconomic indicators of Angola.

Table 3.1 Selected Economic Indicators of Angola, 2003 – 2007

	2003	2004	2005	2006	2007
Gross domestic product (current prices, millions of U.S. dollars)	13,956	19,800	30,632	45,167	58,696
Real GDP (%)	3.3	11.2	20.6	18.6	23.4
Oil sector (%)	-2.2	13.1	26.0	13.1	22.3
Non-oil sector (%)	10.3	9.0	14.1	27.5	25.1
Gross National Income (GNI) per person (U.S. dollars)	848	1,157	1,740	2,506	3,180
Inflation Rate (consumers prices %)	106.00	76.60	43.80	23.00	13.20
Nominal External[1] debt (81.0 in 2002) %	69.0	48.6	37.6	28.8	22.2
External debt-to-GDP ratio	73.1	54.5	39.9	20.3	16.3

Compiled by the Author
Sources: IMF (http://www.imf.org/external/np/sec/pn/2007/pn07115.htm), World Development Indicators database, September 2008 and CIA World Factbook 2007 (https://www.cia.gov/library/publications/the-world-factbook/)

[1] The nominal value of a debt instrument is the amount that at any moment in time the debtor owes to the creditor at that moment; this value is typically established by reference to the terms of a contract between the debtor and creditor.

The economic indicators of Angola improved dramatically following the end of the civil war in 2002. The Angola' economic and financial program achieved significant progress toward macroeconomic stability as a result of the solid implementation of key program measures, supported by a rebound in oil prices. Foreign reserves are being rebuilt, and the fiscal position is improving, aided by expenditure adjustment (IMF 2010).

Recent literature describes economic growth as a means toward enhanced human development (Ranis and Stewart 2001). Economic growth is an important factor in reducing poverty and generating the resources necessary for human development. The time series in Table 3.1 clearly demonstrates that there has been economic growth in Angola since the end of the civil war.

Therefore, the imperative of economic growth could underpin sustainable human development in post-conflict Angola. At a macro-level, the distribution of the increased income from economic growth would have a strong impact on human development. Since poorer households spend a higher proportion of their income on goods that directly promote better health and education, economic growth whose benefits are directed more toward the poor will have a greater impact on human development, via increased food expenditure as well as on education.

As Table 3.1 shows, the key positive aspects of the national output in post-conflict Angola are (1) a sharp increase of the GDP, (2) improvement in the inflation rate, and (3) a decrease in external debt. A critical assessment of these aspects explains the extent to which economic growth in post-conflict Angola presents a major opportunity for reconstruction of Angola.

3.1.1. Increased GDP

Since 2002, Angola has experienced a radical growth on its income. Income growth is described as the main contributor to directly increasing the capabilities of individuals and consequently the human development of a nation since it signals the economy's command over resources (Sen 2001). It is very good sign, as Table 3.1 shows, that the Angolan GDP has grown considerably last few years.

Table 3.2 Angola Nominal GDP in USD Billion (2002-2010)

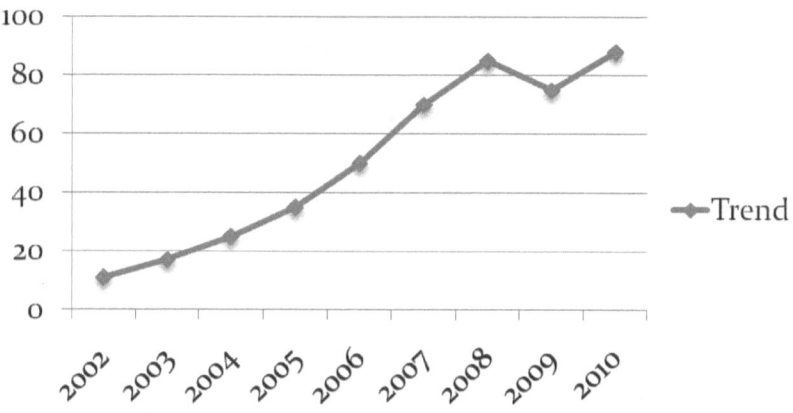

Compiled data from IMF and World Bank

The GDP could have a strong effect on literacy and health outcomes, both through private expenditures and government programs. It is much more encouraging that the real GDP has increased from 3.3 percent in 2003 to 85 percent in 2010 and the GNI[58] per capita went from $848 in 2003 to $3,180 in 2007. These increases further symbolize the extent to which Angola experienced economic growth.

There is a strong connection between GNI per capita and indicators of development such as life expectancy, infant mortality, adult literacy, and political and civil rights (Ranis 2004). As Anand and Ravallion (1993) demonstrate, most of the effects of economic growth on human development are likely to flow through government budgetary expenditures. However, the power of these effects depends entirely on the effectiveness of expenditure targeting and delivery. The reasons that may prevent the economic growth from promoting human development are discussed later in this chapter. Following are key sectors that contribute to the national output in post-conflict Angola.

The Oil Sector

Angola's economic performance is mainly determined by the amount of oil production, which accounts for over 90 percent of exports

(Magubane 2008). The government-owned company (Sociedade Nacional de Combustíveis de Angola—SONANGOL) is responsible for oil exploration and production. The country is one of Africa's biggest oil producing countries—it is also considered one of the world's most exciting oil exploration prospects.

After becoming a member of Organization for the Petroleum Exporting Countries (OPEC) in late 2006, Angola was assigned a production quota of 1.9 million barrels a day, somewhat less than the 22.5 million barrels Angola's government had wanted. Accordingly, this sub-section first re-examines the extent to which oil plays a major role in Angolan macroeconomic situation. Then it critically analyses to what extent the 2008 up and down in global oil prices affects the economic growth in Angola.

Table 3.3. Angola's Oil Production and Consumption, 1999 – 2009

Source: EIA International Energy Annual; Short-Term Energy Outlook

In 2006, oil production increased by about 12.6 percent to reach nearly 514 million barrels compared with about 456 million barrels in 2005. The oil sector has benefited enormously from a number of new discoveries, placing Angola in the coveted position of having the largest reserve growth in the world and first place among the world's top fifteen oil finders (USGS 2007). As Table 3.3 shows, Angola's oil consumption is relatively small. However, oil consumption is expected to increase as Angola's infrastructure is refurbished and expanded.

According to World Bank reports, most of the major international oil companies have acquired interests in Angola, including British Petroleum (BP), Chevron Corporation and Exxon Mobil Corporation of the United States, Eni S.p.A of Italy, Royal Dutch Shell group of the Netherlands, and Total S.A. of France (World Bank Group 2006). In 2006, Angola was producing about 1.4 million barrels per day (Mbbl/d) of oil; its production continues to increase. Despite limitations imposed by OPEC, companies operating in Angola are on track to significantly ramp up their offshore developments in the short and medium term. Industry analysts have estimated that Angolan production capacity could peak between 2.5 and 3 million bb/d by 2015 based on existing discoveries (USGS 2006).

Oil production and its supporting activities constitute the main Angolan exports as well as contribute about 80 percent of the GDP. The Angolan economy will experience a massive oil revenue bonus with a simultaneous fiscal gain during the next two decades or so (World Bank 2007). This is a positive factor for sustaining economic growth in post-conflict Angola.

Empirical evidence shows that Sub-Saharan Africa has made remarkable economic progress since 2000. Its average annual growth rate increased from 3.7 percent in 1996-2000 to 6.3 percent in 2003–2007; at the same time its inflation declined from 18.8 percent to 8.2 percent (Osakwe 2007). However, there was concern that the 2008–9 global financial crisis[59] could disrupt the economic growth in the region. Nevertheless, the impact of the global financial crisis varied across countries depending on their production and export structures—exposure to the international financial system—as well as their capacity to moderate the potential negative effects of the crisis. For example, African countries with relatively low inflation, such as Angola, could use monetary policy to reduce the impact of the crisis on real variables since in this case monetary policy is not constrained by the need to fight inflation.

As Table 3.4 shows, from 2004 to 2008, Angola has enjoyed a sharp increase in oil prices.

Table 3.4. Weekly Angola Cabinda Spot Price FOB

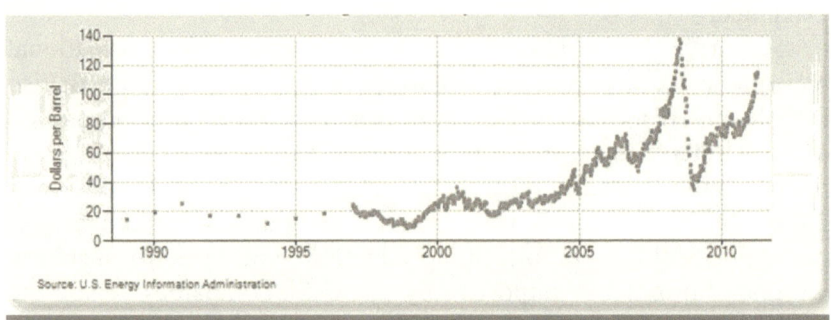

Source: U.S. Energy Information Administration

http://www.eia.doe.gov/dnav/pet/hist/LeaflIandler.ashx?n=PET&s=WEPCAOCAB&f=W

The oil boom provides the Angolan government with important financial revenues that can be invested in rebuilding social infrastructures capable of promoting development and fightingpoverty.

The global financial crisis has obviously affected the crude oil international market. There has been roughly a $100-a-barrel collapse in oil prices in market since July 2008. The state members of OPEC, the reliant of oil revenues, were concerned at the extent to which prices have fallen. As a result, in its monthly report, OPEC reduced its forecast for 2009 demand by 190,000 barrels a day to 690,000, which was its seventh-consecutive forecast reduction.

No country was fully exempted from the international financial crisis. However, the degree of effects is different from one country to another. While for some the international financial crisis caused major economic disruption, some were trying hard to find the ways and means to resist the crisis. In Angola, the prices of oil fell from $137 dollars per barrel in July 2008 to $37 dollars per barrel in December of the same year as a result of financial crisis. The Angolan Council of Ministers in January 2009 confirmed that the country was affected by the international financial crisis.

It is obvious that the fall of oil prices was a major blow for Angola, the country that intended to boost its economic state in order to rebuild its socioeconomic infrastructures devastated by the twenty-seven years of civil war. However, in order to have a critical understanding of the extent to which the fall of oil prices affected economic growth in Angola, it is important to do a time series of the annual oil prices compare to production growth.

Despite the up and down of oil prices during the 2008, the annual average curve of oil prices in Angola has increased since 2002. Moreover, as shown in Table 3.3, the production of oil in Angola has been rapidly increasing since the end of conflict. Angola produced roughly two million barrel of crude oil a day in 2008, more than a double of daily production in 2002. The rapid increase of daily production of oil and average annual prices signify that Angola's national output is still growing. Angola now sells more daily barrels of oil at high price than before 2002.

Compared to Nigeria, another giant oil producer in Africa, the situation of Angola is even encouraging. There has been a higher demand for heavier Angolan crude oil grades like Dalia and Hungo than for lighter gasoline crude like Nigeria's Qua Iboe, due to the drop in U.S. demand for fuel in the wake of the economic downturn in 2008–9. The concise loading program is only going to increase the demand for Angolan oil, which has done quite well considering the slump in world demand (Johnson and Brock 2009). The 2008 rise and fall of international oil prices have surely disturbed the Angolan economy's cadence, but it did not halt considerably its economic growth. This signifies that despite international financial crisis, Angola had the ingredients to further stimulate its economic growth. Nonetheless, in order to maintain long-term economic growth, it is encouraging that Angola uses some of revenues from oil to invest in non-extraction sectors.

The Diamond Sector

The diamond sector is the second major contributor to Angola's national output and constitutes the country's second-largest foreign exchange earner. Alluvial and Eluvial diamond deposits occur in the Provinces of Cunene, Huambo Bie, Kuando Kubango, Kwanza Sul, Lunda, Malange, Moxico, Huila, and Uige. The country hosts intensive diamond reserves, principally in the province of Lunda Norte and Lunda Sul. About 700 kimberlite pipes containing reserves of about 50 million carats are known to exist in the country. Other deposits are thought to occur in coastal areas and offshore (IDRC 2005).

The long civil war undermined the pace of exploitation of its considerable metals and minerals base. Moreover, prior to 2002, diamonds contributed little to the Angola national output as these were largely controlled by UNITA. In 2000, UNITA was estimated to have earned US$150 million from illegal diamond mining, while the informal sector diamond diggers earned US$240 million.[60] In late 2001, a UN monitoring panel reported that more than US$1 million worth of diamonds was leaving Angola illegally daily (Magubane 2008). Of these, UNITA was thought to be responsible for between 25 to 30 percent, the rest smuggled from areas taken over by government troops (Dietrich 2004).

With the end of the war, the government has been able to exert control over diamonds,[61] which make up most of Angola's remaining exports after oil, with yearly production of 6 million carats (USGS 2006). Diamond production is also projected to increase significantly. To attract foreign companies to Angola, the country's first diamond polishing was set up in 2005 as a joint project between government-owned diamond company (Empresa Nacional de Diamantes de Angola—ENDIAMA) and Israeli diamond magnate, Lev Leviev (BMI 2008). According to the Angola Mining Report for the second quarter of 2008, at least ten companies were engaged in diamond exploration and/or production in Angola in 2008.[62] ENDIAMA is responsible for creating partnerships with international companies prospecting for diamonds and is a partner in all diamond ventures (Dietrich 2004).

Sociedade de Comercialização de Diamantes de Angola (SODIAM), which is in charge of the marketing, sale, and trade of all diamond produced in Angola, is comprised of ENDIAMA subsidiaries. It is also the entity responsible for Kimberley Process compliance—ENDIAMA Prospeção e Produção S.A.R.L., which oversees all ENDIAMA's mining and prospecting interests (Dietrich 2004). Diamond production increased by 29.6 percent to reach 9,175 carats compared with 7,079 carats in 2005. In 2006, Angola ranked seventh among the world's leading producers of rough diamond by volume and fifth in terms of value.

However, the World Bank suggests that Angola's diamond sector remains secretive. Improvements will depend on the implementation of a predictable and transparent legal framework that adequately defines the rights and obligations of investors and guarantees tenure rights to investors upon obtaining a mining permit, and on the government's success in liberalizing the market and monitoring and regulating the sector (USGS 2006).

The Non-Diamond and Non-Oil Sector

Even though not developed, the non-diamond and non-oil sector bring some contributions to the national output in Angola. Before the independence, Angola was a major producer of iron ore, gold, and copper.[63] Unlike the colonial era, since the independence of Angola, the contribution of non-oil and non-diamond sector to the national output has been very small (Vines 2005). The rapid settler exodus, wholesale nationalization, and the emergence of civil war had deteriorated the non-oil and non-diamond sector. The war limited most non-resource economic activity to a coastal region, mainly around Luanda, with other urban centers sustained by oil money and donor assistance.

The countryside, where UNITA was dominant, relied on subsistence agriculture. In some less war-affected provinces, such as Huíla, some agricultural activities and small businesses emerged in the 1990s.[64] The post-war reconstruction and resettlement of returnees has contributed to high rates of growth in construction and agriculture. Subsistence agriculture provides the main livelihood for most people but as noted in the preceding chapter, half of the country's food is still imported.

***

Angola has the potential to make a smooth transition from poverty to sustainable human development if the country's abundant natural resources are well managed. Diamond and oil revenue can help to regenerate the agriculture and industry sectors, which can boost the social economic situation of Angola. The increased production of oil, as well as mining, which has contributed to the rise in per capita income in the country, can enable Angola to finance projects for reconstruction of socioeconomic infrastructure for sustainable human development.

3.1.2. Improved Inflation Rate

The rate of inflation in Angola has been decreasing dramatically since the end of the war. This symbolizes another positive element of economic growth in post-conflict Angola. Often inflation creates uncertainty about the future, as there are costs of having to cope with inflation (Burda and Wyplosz 2005). Inflation provokes a rise in the wide-ranging level of prices of goods and services over a period of time.[65] It erodes the real purchasing-power of fixed payments unless they are inflation-adjusted to keep their real values constant. Empirical and academic evidence prove a high level of inflation has negative implications on the living conditions of people, thereby provoking poor human development (Hall and Taylor 1991).

Table 3.5. Inflation in Post-Conflict Angola

	2002	2003	2004	2005	2006	2007	2008	2009	2010
Trend	105,6	76,7	31	18,5	12,2	11,78	13,18	13,99	15,31

Compiled data from IMF and World Bank

The falling inflation rate in Angola represents a positive factor in the fight against poverty. Low inflation enables the stability of economy. It permits consumers and businesses to make long-term plans because they know that their money is not losing its purchasing power year after year. It encourages lower interest rates (both in nominal and real terms) that encourage investment to improve productivity and allowing businesses to prosper without raising prices. Thus, low inflation has the potential to contribute to the financial security of both householders and businesses in Angola.

To stabilize the economy and avoid major economic shocks, such as the Great Depression, governments must make adjustments through policy changes. These adjustments are necessary to maintain stability and continue growth. This economic management is achieved through two types of strategies: fiscal policy and monetary policy (*Blanchard 2000*). What financial and monetary policies of the Angolan government contributed to lowering inflation in post conflict?

Since the end of the civil war, the Angolan government has improved its fiscal and monetary policies. Since September 2003, Angola has adopted an anti-inflation policy that has led to a sharp decline in inflation—from about 100 percent in mid-2003 to about 12 percent at year end 2007. The consumer price index increased by 12 percent in 2006 and 11.8 percent in 2007.

The fiscal policy adopted by the Angolan government since the end of the conflict has succeeded in reducing the rate of inflation. The Angolan government began financing its fiscal deficit with oil-backed loans that also supplied the country's national bank (Banco Nacional de Angola—BNA) with foreign exchange to stabilize the exchange rate (Gasha 2004). Nonetheless, even though the inflation rate declined rapidly, it overshot the government's targets in 2004, 2005, and 2006, and remains above the average for other oil exporters in sub-Saharan Africa (IMF 2007). Moreover, recent economic developments show that inflation is stagnating, after declining to 11.7 percent in the twelve months ending in March 2008; inflation for the twelve months ending in July 2008 reached 12.5 percent, the highest rate since a peak of 12.68 percent in July 2006.

The increased oil revenues and prudent macroeconomic policies contributed to stabilization of the nominal exchange rate in post-conflict Angola (OCED 2007). After depreciating reasonably in 2004, the kwanza (Angolan currency) appreciated in nominal terms in both 2005 and 2006; it then stabilized at about the level it reached when the "hard-kwanza policy" began in 2003 (Economist Intelligence Unit 2005). The real effective exchange rate index rose by a cumulative 50 percent between 2003 and 2006. Since 2002, there have been considerable variations across the different monetary aggregates. Following a slow rise in 2003–4, monetary aggregate growth rose in 2005 then slowed again in 2006 (IMF 2007).

The growth of broad money[66] was about 60 percent in 2006 after following the same path as base money through 2005. The monetary aggregate framework centers on a stable relationship between money and national income. However, this correlation between money and national income appears to change with remonetization as consumer confidence improves after a period of high inflation (Friedman 2005).

The rapid accumulation of foreign exchange earnings has allowed the government to intervene through open-market operations, stabilize the kwanza's nominal exchange rate against the dollar, and dampen inflationary pressures. The improvement in fiscal outcomes so far has been due to increases in oil revenue (IMF 2007). Moreover, exchange rate-based stabilization policies entail additional costs such as currency appreciation, which detracts from the competitiveness of domestically produced tradable goods (AfDB/OECD 2006).

The current Angola monetary framework, which is anchored to base money targeting and has helped to restrain inflation, should stand, but it should be adjusted to incorporate all measures of dollarization and be complemented by other indicators. The exchange rate should be more flexible to allow it to appreciate nominally in the event that inflationary pressures arise. Additional work to modify the measures of currency in circulation, to conduct more sophisticated tests to assess the relationship between inflation and the monetary aggregates, and to determine how to include the currency measure in monetary operations is needed. Developing more reliable and timely data would also help policymakers to better test the stability of money demand in Angola. Moreover, it should be noted that the domestic economy consists mostly of non-tradable services. Furthermore, all these costs must be weighed against the fiscal benefits, in terms of improved tax collection brought about by the decline in inflation.

Angola needs reliable statistics on several aspects of economic activity, including the determinants of demand for the monetary aggregates, such as nominal GDP and prices (Gasha 2005). The problems are on both sides of the equation; broad money does not capture all money. The absence of reliable time series data has prevented the authorities from analyzing in-depth the main characteristics of the macroeconomic and the financial system (IMF 2007). Despite some improvements in fiscal and monetary policies, a great deal of more progress is needed to achieve transparency concerning oil revenues.

Angola has subscribed to the Extractive Industry Transparency Initiative, but de-facto implementation has been limited.[67]

3.1.3. Decreased External Debts

Prior to 2002, Angola was heavily indebted due to the high cost of war. However, the country dramatically has reduced its external debt (including arrears and late interest) since the end of civil war. As a result of rising oil prices and production, the ratio of nominal external debt to GDP declined from 73.1 percent at the end of 2003 to 16.3 percent at the end of 2007. As Bohn (1988) argues, nominal debt provokes fluctuations in the budgets. Any external nominal debt creates an incentive for the government to increase inflation and reduces welfare (Barro and Gordon 1983). Therefore, the fact that Angola has decreased radically its nominal external debt is a positive incentive for economic growth and human development.

The IMF projected in 2005 that Angola's external debt was sustainable in the long run, citing increased government revenue from oil production.[68] With more oil production scheduled, prospects are promising for continued economic growth and strong public finances.[69] In October 2006, the World Bank report that Angola's external debt-to-GDP ratio was expected to decline sharply due to the expected rapid growth in GDP. In this context, the management of Angola's debt does not appear oppressive (IMF 2007). Indeed, Angola could choose to pay off debts outright. Therefore, the issue is not necessarily debt forgiveness, but rather the terms under which Angola will terminate its debt.

The Angola government is focusing its debt liquidation efforts on its obligations to Paris Club[70] members. It has already paid Paris Club creditors all its arrears except late interests and has resumed the normal payment of the maturities of its outstanding debt. This formal commitment from Angola to clear all its remaining arrears with Paris Club creditors allows Angola to improve its credit worthiness, diversify its sources of financing, and obtain better rates on commercial loans. This can further contribute to economic growth in the post-conflict era and consequently improve the living conditions of citizens.

In the short run, the Angolan government's rapid payment of the country's external debts may add challenges to the government's ability to deliver emergent and basic services to people. Given the fact that Angolan debts were accumulated during decades of civil war, rapid repayment can divert large sums of money that could otherwise be allocated into projects of rebuilding social-economic infrastructure capable of sustaining human development. However, in the long run, a debt-free Angolan government would have less dependence on external donors and would have autonomy in deciding how to use the national revenues—subsequently investing in rebuilding social infrastructures capable of improving the living conditions of people.

Increased GDP, low inflation rate, and decreased external debt constitute incentives to economic growth that could play a major role in sustaining human development in post-conflict Angola. The growing of the GDP per capita contributes to rising government revenue, which could encourage social investments to improve the living condition of people. The low inflation rate incites households and businesses' trust in commodity, financial, and labor markets. Stable markets can attract investments and create jobs and an environment for sustainable human development (Mueller 2001).

Summary

The economic indicators of Angola improved dramatically following the end of the civil war in 2002. The country is making remarkable leaps toward improving its national output. The key positive aspects of the national output in post-conflict Angola are a sharply increasing of the GDP, improvement in the inflation rate, and a decrease in external debt. Economic growth will enable Angola to rebuild socioeconomic infrastructures (roads, bridges, dams) and improve its communications and other vital systems, which are crucial for human development.

However, serious questions can be raised about the efficiency of infrastructure investment decisions in post-conflict Angola. The cost of infrastructure programs, especially for projects that do not reflect the priority of local communities, can divert funds away from other investments. The infrastructure investment can squeeze other priorities; therefore, the Angola government needs to identify urgent projects that will tangibly respond to the current needs of poor Angolans. Moreover, another question of infrastructure investment in Angola is the fact it creates enclaves in a few provinces. The majority of infrastructure projects are situated in coastal regions, chiefly Luanda, and the interior is widely neglected.

The fact that the investment in Angola is focused on the oil sector presents a potential danger for economic growth to reverse if the production diminished. The oil sector is extremely technological. Therefore, the improvement of the investment climate is the key to releasing long-term growth and prosperity. The Angolan government should reform its economic policies and encourage diversification of businesses capable of creating jobs, as well as making basic social investments that are capable of empowering the poor. Only an improved investment climate will attract the small businesses and foreign investment that can create new jobs and contribute to the well-being of people. Economic and political factors are intertwined. Economic growth can lift the living conditions of people in Angola only if there is political will.

IV. THE IMPACT OF ECONOMIC GROWTH ON HUMAN DEVELOPMENT IN ANGOLA

The preceding chapter explained the extent to which the growth of GDP per capita, decreased inflation, and diminution of external debt contribute to economic growth in post-conflict Angola. However, the impact of economic growth on human development also depends on other conditions within society. One important aspect here is the role of the distribution of income, both at a micro level within a household as well as at a macro level across households. At the micro level there is great potential for a positive causality; people's consumption can be an important element in increasing human development and may respond more closely to the real needs of the population than do government programs.

However, individual consumption may not always go toward goods that contribute significantly to human development. In societies where women contribute more to family income and have more influence on household decision-making, expenditures on human development-oriented goods are likely to be relatively higher. (Clark 2006, 2008).

The government budgetary expenditure is critical to the attempt to transfer economic growth to human development (Anand and Ravallion 1993). The effectiveness of public expenditure is conditional on the quality of governance, with government accountability likely to play an important role. The government needs to identify priority sectors that have the highest potential for human development improvement. Moreover, government expenditures for human development should be distributed predominantly to low income groups and should also have the institutional capacity to efficiently allocate these expenditures. Therefore, this chapter analyses, among others, which economic dilemmas the Angolan government is facing for the transfer of economic growth into sustainable human development.

To sustain human development, national macroeconomics situation requires a well-functioning commodity, financial, and labor market (Layard, Nickell, and Jackman 2005). As explained in the preceding chapter, the Angolan commodity market is dominated by the export of raw material and the import of finished goods. Abundance of natural resources in Angola attracts the investment of foreign companies that contribute to the sustainability of the commodity market. In addition, the extensive revenue from the oil trade and other raw materials enables Angola to balance its financial market. However, as shown in Chapter II, the labor market in Angola is poor. The country has high unemployment, and the majority of the population is operating in informal markets. As a result, households do not have financial security to pay for their basic needs or taxes. Hence, the Angolan national budget relies mainly on corporation taxes and foreign financial loans to function.

The labor market suffers from a severe shortage of skilled personnel at all levels. The situation is particularly uncertain with respect to technical staff. Reductions in investment in education were significant during the time of civil war, and it is estimated that 50 percent of Angolans do not have formal nor informal professional skills (Bjerke 2004). Companies and institutions generally refer to the lack of skilled and educated personnel as the major limitation that impedes the impact of investments—posing an extra risk and cost to investors. Weak management capacity is another serious effect of this situation (Bjerke 2004). The following sections analyze the contrast between economic growth and human development, exploring the circumstance under which economic growth can generate prosperity in post-conflict Angola.

4.1. Natural Resource Curse

Many developing countries possess significant reserves of oil and other natural resources. Numerous academic studies show that countries that are highly dependent on revenues from oil and other minerals score lower on the UNDP's Human Development Index. Moreover, such wealth often fuels internal criticism that causes conflict and corruption. This pattern is widely referred to as the "natural resource curse"[71] or "Dutch disease"[72] (Poelhekke and Van Der Ploeg 2007).

The natural resource curse is clearly illustrated in Angola, where a rapid economic growth boosted by oil boom has not yet reflected on human development. Angola has limited capacity to record accurately the huge sums of oil money suddenly pouring into the country. This is one of reasons it remains difficult to obtain accurate government statistics. Scholars argue that it is essential that Angola develop the institutional capacity required to manage current and future revenue to sustain its economy (Mai and Wisner 2007).

In September 2002, the British former Prime Minister, Tony Blair, announced the Extractive Industries Transparency Initiative (EITI) at the World Summit on Sustainable Development in Johannesburg. The main objective of the EITI was to establish voluntary compacts between governments and companies regarding natural resource revenue transparency. Using standardized reporting templates, companies would report what they pay governments and state agencies, including state-owned oil companies and provincial governments.[73] The EITI has some strength as it enlarges the scope of reporting coverage to include state oil companies and government. However, its major weakness is that it is a voluntary compact, allowing some states to resist participating on it.

Angola offers a key example of how countries rich in oil can suffer, albeit in changing degrees, in economic development and political stability because of the very commodity that they perceive as their greatest hope. The apparently guaranteed continuous boom of oil revenue gives the government a disincentive to spend productively, stimulate diversity in the domestic economy and its exports, and establish a system of checks and balances that will make it easier for the government to borrow at reasonable rates.

However, Angola is less concerned about conditional loans as it is earning billions from oil and has access to non-unconditional loans from China. Moreover, because the government needs to spend now, it borrows from international banks at high rates and relies on oil-backed loans from export-import banks. The outcome is an extremely inefficient allocation of resources, with a large portion of oil revenue going to finance loans at high rates of interest (IMF 2006). High GDP from oil revenue can hide serious problems in a country's economy, such as high unemployment.

The major question is how to keep governments of oil-rich developing states from engaging in corrupt acts and manipulating economic growth and political stability in their countries. Putting international pressure to promote transparency in the transactions between multinational oil companies and host-governments is a logical way, but it is not easy task. International and national organizations' pressure campaigns directed at the oil industry can only go so far.

Individually, oil companies will not voluntarily publish what they pay to Angola, unless they are forced to do so universally. The prospect of universal regulation is very limited but worth exploring, especially the prospect of global cooperation between securities commissions to implement consistent disclosure rules for resource extraction companies (Arezki and Van Der Ploeg 2007).

The natural resource curse represents an enormous impediment to human development in post-conflict Angola. There is not enough transfer from the Angolan economy boom into social investments. The negative effects of "Dutch disease" produced by large inflows of foreign exchange are one of major challenges facing attempts to sustain human development in post-conflict Angola. Improving this institutional failure requires changes of law and practice but does not require huge resource investments.

Lifting the natural resource curse would be a major economic prospect for Angola. It would help ensure that existing resources are used efficiently, and the resulting improvement in the economic atmosphere would attract additional resources, making for better growth prospects. Therefore, to fully take advantage of its rich national resources, Angola will need to implement government reforms and increase transparency.

4.1.1. Doing Business in Post-Conflict Angola

Considering its huge natural resources and geographical position, Angola presents various opportunities for business. Flourishing business opportunities can contribute to the creation of jobs, which would provide households with financial security to pay for their basic needs (such as food, education, electricity, health care, and water), as well as pay taxes to the government (if a taxation system exists). It was difficult to do business properly in Angola during three decades of civil war in Angola. The most dominant business during that era was the trade in arms and natural resources (IRIN 2008). With the end of war, it is important to explore the existing dilemmas of doing business in Angola.[74]

Angola participates in a number of trade agreements and is a member of regional trade agreements, including the Southern African Development Community (SADC) and the Common Market for Eastern and Southern Africa (COMESA). Moreover, Angola benefits from non-reciprocal preferential treatment from many industrialized countries under the Generalized System of Preferences (GSP), including the European Union's Everything But Arms (EBA) initiative and the United States' Africa Growth and Opportunity Act (AGOA).

Angola is also a signatory to the Cotonou Agreement, and together with some members of SADC, it negotiated a reciprocal Economic Partnership Agreement (EPA) with the European Union (EU) that will replace the Cotonou Agreement. However, Angola has slowly taken advantage of these preferential arrangements because of its lack of capacity to produce and its lack of competitiveness (Integrated Framework 2005). However, the dependence of Angolan economy on oil revenues makes economic diversification difficult as investments flow to oil or oil-related sectors.

Angola has created a national agency for private investment (Agência Nacional para o Investimento Privado—ANIP),[75] but until 2010, the country was still ranked near the bottom of the World Bank's Doing Business Index (168 out of 181 countries).[76] Since its creation in 1976, SONANGOL was protected from the dominant logic of Angola's political economy. By the time Angola adopted a multiparty system in the early 1990s; SONANGOL was the key domestic actor in the economy.

Loans for SONANGOL or general government access oil-backed credit lines—used by countries such as Portugal, Brazil, and China—have provided guarantees for foreign companies doing business in Angola. The result has been a fairly effective (if expensive) delivery of large projects, such as the Capanda hydroelectric dam[77] built partly by Brazil's company, Odebrecht. Thus, Angola allocates oil cargoes to the Brazilian government, which pays Odebrecht directly for its work in Angola (Vines et al. 2005).

Nonetheless, the growing complexity of SONANGOL has not led to successful development. Instead, SONANGOL has primarily provided a key tool for elite empowerment (Oliveira 2007). Therefore, the impact of Angola's newborn prosperity is not widespread because the increased capital resources have not been channeled effectively into productive public and private sector investments. Angola's elites emphasize their interest in private investment, but they have yet to make the country sufficiently open, in the view of many investors. Favoritism and the labyrinthine bureaucracy that businesses must navigate to have a profit frighten away some investors (Oliveira 2007).

According to the World Bank, Angola is among the most difficult places in the world to do business.[78] The Angolan government strictly regulates business start-up and employment. Property registration is difficult, and contract enforcement is inefficient. There is a lot to be done to make Angola more attractive to foreign and domestic investors. With an increasingly integrated global economy, investors have a variety of choices about where to invest, and Angola may lose its influence (Mai and Wisner 2007). Some financiers around the world will not invest until Angola's business climate improves both in absolute terms and relative to its neighbors (World Bank 2007). This situation has a negative impact on sustainable economic growth and human development.

4.1.2. Angola-China Business Relations

The diplomatic relationship with China has become one of Angola's most successful businesses. Commercial trade between China and Angola has grown remarkably in recent years. Bilateral trade volume between China and Angola reached 25.3 billion USD in 2008, making Angola China's largest trading partner in Africa and its single largest source of oil (Ian 2006). Together, the United States and China share 60 percent of Angolan oil exports.[79] Chinese imports to Angola have sharply increased since 2003. In 2004, China became Angola's fourth-largest trading partner at $194 million, up from being its seventh largest trading partner the year before. In 2006, China kept its position despite the fact that Chinese exports to Angola quadrupled, with steel and iron bars, batteries, cement, and automobiles as the principal imports (Campos and Vines 2008).

In early 2007, China surpassed Brazil and South Africa as the second-largest trading partner behind Portugal. Imports reached $368 million, an increase of 106 percent from the same period the year before. Oil exports to China have increased since 2002. China has extended three multibillion dollar lines of credit to the Angolan government—two loans of $2 billion from China Exim Bank, one in 2004, the second in 2007, as well as one loan in 2005 of $2.9 billion from China International Fund Ltd. (Hanson 2008). The two loans from China Exim Bank finance projects on energy, water, health, education, fisheries, and communications.

The $2.9 billion credit line, which is managed by Angola's Reconstruction Office, Gabinete de Reconstrução Nacional (GRN),[80] is allocated for railway rehabilitation, highway construction, and building a new airport. Unlike projects undertaken by the ministry of finance, it is unclear how much money is directly managed by GRN, how funds are allocated among projects, and how much money has so far been spent (Shaxson 2008). Some analysts are worried by the fact that the Angolan government has grown closer to China at the expense of its other diplomatic relationships (Campos and Vines 2008). Nonetheless, Western oil companies still have large business interests in Angola, and Angola need to expand its ties with a variety of countries.

The Angolan government is in favor of China loans because China offers better conditions than commercial loans, lower interest rates, and longer repayment time (Huse 2008). Chinese companies pursue construction deals in Angola because there is limited competition (Campos and Vines 2008). A Chinese official said that the Chinese brigades have been working day and night so that by the end of 2011, the rehabilitation of Lobito (Benguela) railways up to Luau town in the eastern Moxico Province can be concluded in order to benefit Angolan development (Angola Press 2008).

However, critics have argued that the massive movement of Chinese and foreigners workers in Angola are taking jobs away from Angolans. Experts doubt the Angolan government's ability to maintain Chinese projects after they are completed (Huse 2008). It must be signalled this promise was not fulfilled. The government will need to have an appropriate attention on planning and organization to ensure the sustainability and maintenance of Chinese completed projects (Campos and Vines 2008). However, as argued earlier, building a more educated and skilled population will take time.

In March 2007, Hangxiao Steel Structure Company Ltd., a Chinese construction company, came under investigation by the China Securities Regulatory Commission (CSRC) for suspected stock price rigging in deals related to Angola (China Economic Net 2007). Doubt around the company followed a statement in February by Hangxiao that it had signed a $4.4 billion contract to sell the China International Fund Ltd. construction products and services for its "Residents' Heaven" public housing projects in Angola. In April of the same year, CSRC fined the Shanghai-listed construction company $52,000 for failing to follow legal procedures in the release of financial information (Campos and Vine 2008).

It was during the 2007 trial of Angolan Security Chief General Fernando Garcia Miala that allegations of mismanagement of Chinese funds further emerged. Apparently, General Miala threatened to reveal the names of individuals in senior government positions who had benefited from the diversion of funds from Chinese lines of credit.[81] Some members of the international community, opposition parties, and civil society organizations have raised concerns regarding transparency in the use of Chinese funds for some time (Campos and Vine 2008).

On October 2007, José Pedro de Morais,[82] the former ministry of finance, issued a statement in Luanda denying any misuse of Chinese funds and also publishing details of credit managed by the ministry. Even though the publication of such a report is a positive development, more disclosure is needed, especially regarding the Angolan government, as many of the larger Chinese infrastructure projects are managed out of that office.

4.2. Challenge to Consolidate Human Development in Angola

The major question in post-conflict Angola is how the economic growth can be transformed into sustainable human development. There are mixed opinions on the government's efforts to promote economic diversification and implement a pragmatic development strategy. Some argue that the Angolan government has made significant progress since the end of the war,[83] while others consider that it has not directed enough energy and attention to helping the poor (Hanson 2008).

Graph 4.1

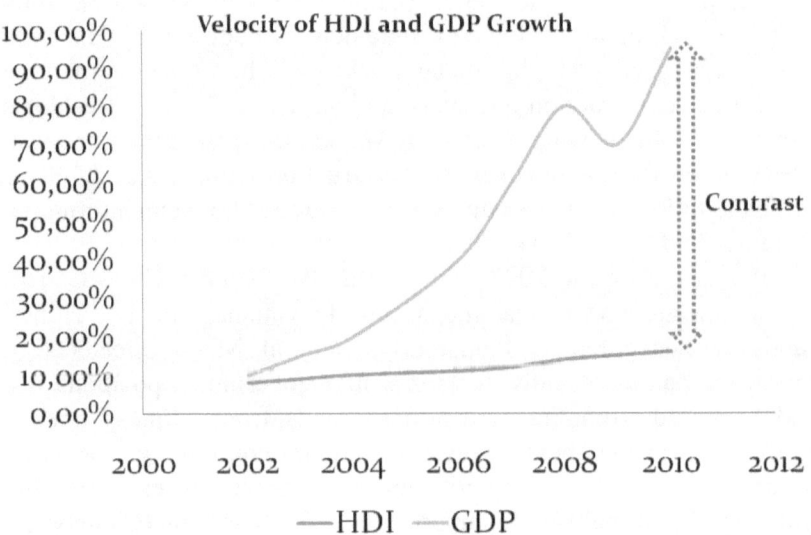

As shown in the graph 4.1, the major contrast is that the Angolan rapid growth of GDP does not reflect the reality of the human development. Though, it is important to recognize that poor human development is a result of both current and historic factors. Apart from the economic ills inherited from Portuguese colonial legacy, Angola was confronted with major political factors that posed a big challenge to human development in the post-independence era. Cold War geopolitics and violent civil war following the independence had widespread implications on deterioration of living conditions of people prior to 2002. Following the independence in 1975, the Angolan government did not have any time to settle in as the war started. The country's large budget spending was allocated to efforts of war. Thus, there was less money to invest in rebuilding social infrastructures.

As a result, the speed of both GDP and human development before 2002 was stagnating.

Although the velocity curve of the GDP has sharply increased since the end of war in 2002, that of human development remains perpendicularly down. As the analysis in Chapter II shows, major social indicators such as life expectancy, malnutrition, and access to water and sanitation deteriorated sharply during the war and are still at alarming levels. The rate of maternal mortality is still one of the highest in the world. Malnutrition is an important underlying condition, estimated to affect almost half of Angola's 7.4 million children (OCED 2007). Angola is always ranked under the list of countries with low human development. This raises a lot of doubt about the country's commitment to improving the living conditions of its people.

As the 2007 World Bank reports show, Angola, together with Nigeria and Chad, illustrate the fact that mineral resources do not always determine development success. This justifies the theory of "resource curse," as the rising oil and diamond revenues have not been fully injected into creating better living conditions for the majority of Angolans.

It is evident that the Angolan government is facing an enormous challenge in rebuilding its infrastructure that was destroyed by war. The countryside provinces were devastated during the civil war and have had yet completely connected to the coastal region through transportation and communication systems. This divide, which reflects the historic division between MPLA and UNITA strongholds, creates disparities in public and commercial services, as well as in living standards (Mai and Wisner 2007).

Poor transportation networks impede the delivery of basic goods to the people in some provinces. In addition, land mines still present a major problem to an adequate irrigation system, and with a dearth of equipment, inhibit agricultural production, impeding the growth of a non-oil economy in some provinces. Moreover, broken education and public health systems contribute to a poor quality of life throughout the country.

The living conditions of Angolans are poor, with two-thirds of the population living in poverty on less than \$2 per day.[84] Infant mortality and other measures of quality of life are among the worst in the world.[85]

The results in Chapter II show that fundamental human rights to health, work, and education as well as freedom of expression, association, and movement, which are fundamental for human development, are still poor. Rather than fighting poverty reduction clearly, the Angolan government has focused on large infrastructure and public works projects (Hanson 2008). The mortgages and rental prices in the newly built houses or apartments are very high—making it difficult for the poor, the majority of Angolan population, to have access to pleasant housing. The country has enough money to build private hospitals for those who can afford the fees, but most Angolans struggle to access even basic health care, which lacks trained staff and infrastructure, particularly in rural areas. Private schools collect exorbitant fees to educate the children of the elite while one third of the country's children are outside of the school system.

The labor market is also one of the major challenges in post-conflict Angola, as unemployment in the country stands at around 70 percent (World Bank 2007). The 2006 opinion poll conducted by the International Republic Institute (IRI) in Angola shows that 75 percent of respondents said unemployment was the most important issue facing the country (IRI 2006). Angola's oil boom may help the country to improve its GDP, but it has created few jobs. Though the thousands of construction sites around Luanda demonstrate that the country is rebuilding itself after decades of war, these projects mainly use imported labor from China, Brazil, and other countries. As a result, only a few Angolans have benefited from these job opportunities.

The weak labor market presents an abnormality of circulation at the macroeconomic level that make it difficult to sustain human development in post-conflict Angola despite the increased of GDP per capita, decrease of inflation, and considerable elimination of external debt. Moreover, poor technical capacity has limited the government's ability to enact these projects (Hanson 2008). Therefore, any discussion of financial inconsistencies of the Angolan government must take into consideration the country's limited number of human and institutional capacity.

Experts argue that ministers and deputy ministers are competent, but the low and middle rungs of the civil service are problematic.

The lack of capacity to support the work of ministers and their deputies is often challenging. As Campos and Vines (2008) argue, although the government is making efforts to train people, it would be impracticable to think that they train people as quickly as they can build infrastructures needed for improving the living conditions of people.

Insignificant investment in the non-natural resources sector is also one of the main challenges to human development in post-conflict Angola. While economic diversification could reduce Angola's vulnerability to fluctuations in the oil market and the potential consequences of large inflows of foreign currency from oil business, foreign direct investment has yet to support a variety of economic sectors. Investment remains weak outside the oil sector and industries involved in rebuilding Angola's infrastructure.

Agriculture has suffered the most; the long period of civil war provoked a massive movement of Angola people from the countryside to the coastal cities (mainly Luanda) for safety and work. Hence, agricultural fields and equipment were neglected or destroyed. As a result, Angola now imports approximately half of its food supply.

To facilitate significant commercial agricultural development, recent land reform laws attempt to reconcile overlapping traditional land-use rights, colonial era land claims, and modern land grants. Nonetheless, the agricultural sector is showing the first signs of sustained growth since the end of war (IMF 2006). Reviving this industry, with its huge farming and fishing potential, could create jobs and help to sustain the welfare of the poor, provided that the land does not become concentrated in the hands of a relatively small number of owners (military generals and elites members of the ruling party).

For sure Angola needs to rebuild its infrastructure, improve its communications and other vital systems. However, it also needs to provide tangible improvements to the lives of poor Angolans. The country should reform its economic policies: encourage diversification of businesses capable of creating jobs as well as making basic social investment (such as education and health) that is capable of empowering the poor and sustaining human development.

Speaking at the conference on rural development that took place on May 5, 2009 in Luanda; Filomena Delgado, the secretary of State for Rural Development (SEDER), stressed that the improvement to

Human Development Index (HDI) in the rural area, through more investments, is one of the priorities of the Angolan government for 2008-2012 period. However, such an ambitious project can be achieved if institutions of 'good governance'[86] are well-established. Hence, as discussed in the following subsection, promoting good governance for human development requires combined efforts of key stakeholders.

To sustain human development in post-conflict Angola will require contributions from various stakeholders, whereby three categories are consider being crucial in this book. State public institutions or government constitute the first category of stakeholders for human development. In countries, like Angola, where electoral processes exist, the state is composed of an elected government and an executive branch. The state's functions are multiple, among others, it is the focus of the social contract that defines citizenship (Adesina 2007). The state has authority to control and use force, responsibility for public services and creating an enabling environment for sustainable human development. The state has responsibility to mediating interests for the public-good as well as provides effective and accountable public services (Mueller 2003).

The challenge faced by states is to ensure that good governance addresses the concerns and needs of the poorest by increasing the opportunities for people to seek, achieve and sustain the type of life they desire. The Angolan government, for example, has received widespread praise about its effort to improve the macroeconomic situation since the end of conflict in 2002. It should, therefore, be prepared to pay attention to voices of those insist that human development is not sustaining.

It is true as, during his speech of 13 April 2009 the Angolan President, José Eduardo dos Santos; insisted on the fact that the major role of the state is guiding, energizing and regulating the people.[87] This means, the first responsibility of the state is to protect the people and provide adequate services. The state, explicitly, has responsibility to do things like upholding the rights of the vulnerable, protecting the environment, maintaining stable macroeconomic conditions, maintaining standards of public health and safety for all at a reasonable cost, mobilizing resources to provide essential public services and infrastructure as well as maintaining order, security and social harmony (Wilson, Kanji and Braathen 2006).

The war in Angola was long—some provinces and people were widely affected than others—some citizens are still traumatized in this post-conflict era. Therefore, State institutions in post-conflict Angola shall find the way to empower the people by providing equal opportunities; ensuring social, economic and political inclusion as well as access to resources. People can be empowered only if their legislatures, electoral processes, legal and judicial systems work properly. Effective legal and judicial systems promote the rule of law and the rights of all. Free and fair elections mean public confidence and trust as well as political legitimacy. Thus, Angola should consolidate its efforts to decentralize political and economic systems to become more responsive to citizens' demands for sustainable human development.

In developed and developing countries alike, the state is being compelled to redefine its role in social and economic activity.[88] Thus, in the attempt of sustaining human development, Angola shall set up mechanism capable to respond to pressures for change from private sector, citizens and international community. To satisfy the private sector, the country needs to provide more conducive market environment as well as a better balance between state and market. To respond to the needs of citizens, there shall be an increased accountability and responsiveness from government, as well as greater decentralization. Finally, Angola shall set up mechanism to resist and adapt the challenging international socioeconomic trends.

The second category of stakeholder for sustainable human development is composed of members of the international community. Of course, the government is the basic player for human development. However, it should be recognized that human development in post-conflict societies, like Angola, would hardly sustain if there is not sufficient and effective support from members of the international community. The international actors for human development encompass foreign governments, UN Agencies and international NGOs (Kumar 2004, French 1999). Although, nation states can be viewed as the major entities in the international system, UN agencies such as the UNDP and regional organizations such the African Union and the European Union also play significant roles in helping countries to build and consolidate Human Development.

The contribution to human development in Angola by some members of the international community was challenging. Cold-

War geopolitics—the interference of Cuba, South Africa's apartheid regime, the former Soviet Union, and the United States in Angola—aggravated violent conflict in the country, causing widespread damage to socioeconomic infrastructures and impeding human development (*Hanhimeaki 2004*). Therefore, considering the direct contribution of foreign actors in the destruction of Angola, the international community should promote moral responsibility to support the country's reconstruction program—help the voices of poor to be heard.

Following the 2002 cease-fire, there have been promises of an international donors' conference where commitments would be made toward reconstructing Angola's war-shattered economy and infrastructure. However, these promises have never been met. Funds pledged in donors' conferences, such as those in Southeast Europe, for example, had helped to boost their socioeconomic development. Some of these countries have moved from aid recipients to donors. In Angola, however, the international community first evoked issues related to good governance and transparency to delay donors' conferences, and then, to avoid the conferences from taking place, they argued that Angola has enough resources to rebuild itself.

The failure to organize a donors' conference for Angola, which could stimulate socioeconomic stability of the country, was a missed opportunity. The delay and refusal by mainly Western countries to assist Angola has encouraged the Angolan government to turn to other partners, such as China, who is now a key player in the post-conflict reconstruction of Angola and whose loans are not bound to conditionality for good governance.

A "stable Angola"[89] has the potential to contribute to the socioeconomic development of Africa and to collective efforts of securing international peace and security, but not to improve the living conditions of its people. The role of members of the international community in Angola, therefore, should not be limited by challenging what the government is doing or not doing. Members of the international community should find ways and means to provide financial as well as technical assistance for Angola to sustain its economic and human development. Of course, UN specialized agencies provide technical assistance to different post-conflict development projects. The efficacy of UN specialized agencies' actions, however, depends on the availability of funds. In the past, relations between the Angolan government and UN, during the time of war, was not good. As a result, one can argue that the UN, in addition of providing technique assistance to Angola, is also cleaning up its image.

As discussed in the preceding chapter, the national output of Angola is better. However, like any other post-conflict society, Angola needs fair and genuine assistance from members of the international community to rebuild the country that experienced such widespread destruction. It is encouraging that in addition to China, Angola's largest trade partner, some countries, including members of the EU, as well as Canada, Japan, and the United States, have shown a commitment to lunch bilateral cooperation with Angola. If effective, this will further boost economic development and subsequently contribute to the improvement living conditions of Angolan people. Nonetheless, this cooperation can only be successful if it is based on mutual respect and win-win principles.

The third category of stakeholder encompasses academic research centers. Existing literature does not link academic research centers to human development. However, the role these institutions play is crucial for sustainable human development. Policies for human development can be drafted through research and action. Research centers are a useful means of knowledge transmission; they are a collection of actors, ideas, and approaches for sustainable human development. However, the majority of universities in Angola do not have research centers. This explains why Angolan scholars find it difficult to publish academic articles or books—therefore contributing little in the search of ideas and strategies for sustainable human development in post-conflict Angola.

The study of human development is multidisciplinary—it requires policy and strategy research, operations research, survey, evaluation, assessment, technical assistance, training, and communication. It needs action in the fields of population, health, education, gender, human resource development, human rights, land, agriculture, rural development, micro-credit, environment, management, and marketing. Research centers can provide expertise on these issues, as well as visualize mainstream studies and technical assistance. Therefore, as a strategy for sustaining human development in post-conflict Angola, the Angolan government and members of the international community should financially assistance Angolan universities to develop different research centers. However, in order for research centers to make visible contributions to national policy, they must be free from political interference and manipulation.

Summary

On the one hand, Angola has made remarkable leaps toward improving its national output, but on the other hand, the country's rapid economic growth has contributed little to attempts to improve the living conditions of poor, which constitute the majority of the Angolan population. The comparison of economic and social indicators shows that there is not enough transfer of the Angolan economic boom into social investments. The speed at which national output and human development grow is often not constant. Macroeconomic indicators can be improved rapidly as a result of steady commodity and financial markets. However, the outcome of social investment, which directly affects human development, can be very slow (Ranis 2000). It is clear that the challenge to rebuild Angola, which experienced devastating civil war, is enormous and will take time. Accordingly, it is important to recognize that the Angolan government is confronted by two issues. On the one hand, there is need to rebuild infrastructure for long-term human development, and on the one hand, there is emergent need to respond to immediate basis needs of people.

It is encouraging that the Angolan government has been injecting Chinese loans into rebuilding socioeconomic infrastructures (roads, bridges, dams) and improve its communications and other vital system, which are crucial for human development. However, serious questions need to be raised about the efficiency of infrastructure investment decisions in post-conflict Angola.

The cost of infrastructure programs, especially for projects that do not reflect the priority of local communities—that is, projects for prestige—can divert funds away from other investments. The infrastructure investment can squeeze other priorities; therefore, the Angolan government needs to identify urgent tangible projects to respond to current needs of poor Angolans. Moreover, another aspect of infrastructure investment in Angola is the fact it creates enclaves in a few provinces. The majority of infrastructure projects are situated in coastal regions, primarily Luanda, and the interior is widely neglected.

The fact that the investment in Angola is focused on the oil sector presents a potential danger for economic growth to reverse if the production diminishes. Thus, the improvement of the investment climate is necessary in order to release long-term growth and prosperity. The Angolan government should reform its economic policies and encourage diversification of businesses capable of creating jobs, as well as make basic social investments that are capable of empowering the poor. Only an improved investment climate will attract the small businesses and foreign investments that can create new jobs and contribute to the well-being of people.

The challenge of sustaining human development in Angola is enormous, which requires a joint-force of the Angolan government, the international community, and academic research centers. The government has the prime responsibility for improving the living conditions of people, as it is the sole organ with power to transform people's demands into policies. However, a post-conflict country, like Angola, requires effective financial and technical support from the international community that can contribute to boosting human development. Moreover, research centers are crucial for human development—as these permit independent and critical studies that can assist policy makers.

External factors, such as oil companies and Chinese business, contribute to the dilemma of fighting corruption and promoting accountability in Angola. Multinational oil companies assisted and backed the mismanagement and misuse of oil revenues by Angolan authorities. The un-conditionality of Chinese loans has encouraged non-transparent, non-accountable governance in Angola. Given the fact that Angola does not largely depend on foreign aid or the donations of international financial institutions such as the World Bank and the International Monetary Fund (IMF) due to large revenue, mainly from its oil boom, it is not obliged to follow the reforms and policy recommendations of such groups. This situation has encouraged an opaque financial system endemic with corruption, which is destabilizing to democratic institutions, thereby contributing to poor human development.

V. THE IMPACT OF POLITICAL
FACTORS ON HUMAN DEVELOPMENT
IN POST-CONFLICT ANGOLA

Angola has enough resources and revenues to contribute to the promotion of sustainable human development in the post-conflict era. The signing of the 2002 Luena Memorandum of Understanding turned a new page for the socioeconomic and political situation in Angola. Large revenues from the oil industry have enabled the Angolan government to dramatically improve the country's macroeconomic indicators. Now the Angolan balance of payment is stable, the GDP per capita has sharply increased, and both inflation and external debts have radically decreased. However, the major contrast is the fact that the rapid growth of national outcome does not correlate with the human development index of Angola; the majority of the people are still living in extreme poverty. Therefore, it crucial to explore what is the main cause of Angola's incapacity to tackle poverty.

As explained in Chapter I, a study of political factors can help explain the quality of the government system's attempts to promote human development. Based on Sen's capability and the UNDP' s participation approaches, it is clear that the concepts "state leadership" and "party system" are crucial in the analysis of governance, as the former guide and the later form the government. The behaviors of state leaders and the ruling parties have major implications for human development. When ruling elites act in favor of good governance, human development has a high chance of sustainability (Smith 2007). Accordingly, among other issues, this chapter analyses to what extent the Angolan ruling party (the MPLA) and its leadership comply with principles of good governance to foster sustainable development.

Dahl (1991) considered democracy a political institution that tends to produce the best feasible system of good governance. Empirical studies prove that democracy correlates with a higher score on the human development index and a lower score on the human poverty index (Blaydes and Kayser 2007). Democratic governments have the potential to put in place better education, longer life expectancy, lower infant mortality, access to drinking water, and better health care than authoritarian systems. This is not due to higher levels of foreign assistance or spending a larger percentage of GDP on health and education but because of good management of available resources (Halperin, Siegle, and Weinstein 2005). Sen (2001) argues that no functioning democracy has ever suffered a large-scale famine and refugee crisis.

Accordingly, the main question in this chapter is to ascertain how the MPLA's government and its leadership's reaction to a wave of democratization have the potential to favor the sustainability of human development in Angola. First, the chapter reassesses the issue of party and state leadership dominance in Angola. Second, it analyses the views of research participants in Angola based on four thematic questions related to democratic governance in post-conflict Angola. Third, it analyses the impasses surrounding the electoral process in Angola.

5.1. Ruling Party and State Leadership Dominance in Post-Conflict Angola

Figure 5.1 splits the post-colonial political background into three waves and summarizes the main characteristics of the three waves of the Angolan post-colonial politics. The first wave (A), or post-Alvor agreement, lasted from 1975 (when Angola received its independence) to 1991 (when the country adopted a multiparty system); the second wave (B), or post-Bicesse Accord wave, commenced in 1991 and lasted until 2002 (when the Angolan civil war ended); and the third wave (C), or Luena memorandum wave, started in 2002. Figure 5.1 illustrates how the dominance of the MPLA and its leadership in power is at the intersection of the three waves of the Angolan post-colonial politics. The question is how the MPLA and its leaders have been surviving the Angola's changing waves.

Figure 5.1 Recapitulation of Waves of Post-Colonial Angola

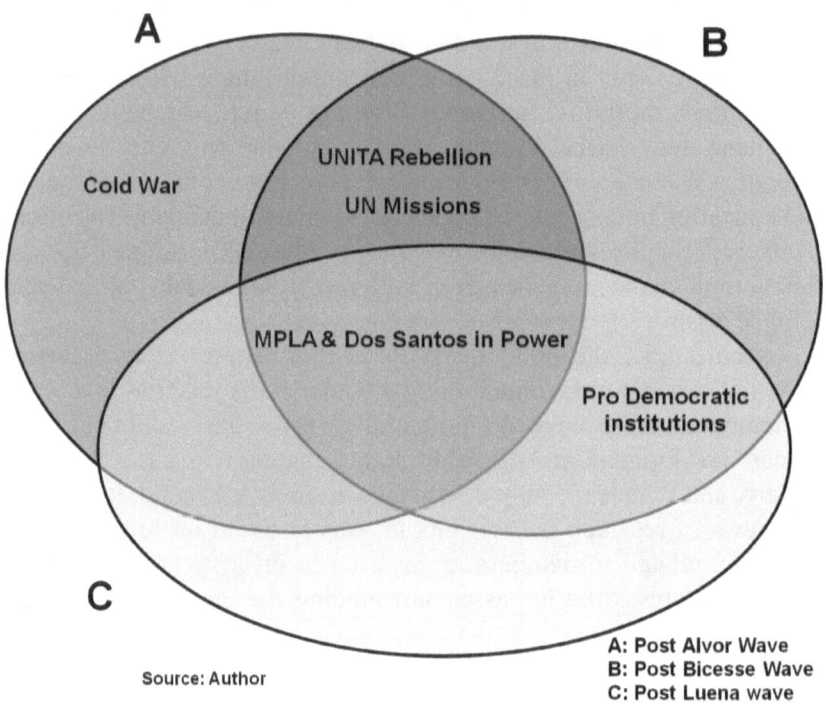

Source: Author

A: Post Alvor Wave
B: Post Bicesse Wave
C: Post Luena wave

The literature shows that the dominance of a ruling party has a negative implication both for attempts to build democracy and sustain human development. Eminent scholars of democratic politics have argued that even though the majority of African countries have enjoyed multiparty elections, there has been no reasonable change in governments (Leftwich 1993).

There is a contradiction between the process of holding multiparty elections in post-Cold War Africa and the quality of leadership they produce, as elected state leaders intend to use all means, even unconstitutional, to hold power (Baker 2002). As a result, rather than promoting democracy and sustaining human development, these leaders are wasting national revenue to build their personal security (Hodges 2004).

With the end of civil war, the only way the MPLA and the president of Angola could reaffirm their legitimacy was through free and fair elections. However, members of opposition parties and civil society in Angola accused the MPLA and its leader of finding political excuses to keep power (Chatta-Chipepa 2003).

Arguably, since President dos Santos came to power in 1979, he has never received a democratic mandate. This is because he never was freely and fairly democratically elected by the Angolan people. When referring to Article 57(2) of the Angolan constitution, Angola could have had its first democratically elected leader if the second round of the presidential election had taken place in 1992, but this did not happen due to renewal of conflict between MPLA and UNITA. The other opportunity for Angolan people to elect democratically was erased in 2010 when the MPLA's dominated parliament changed the national constitution to allow the president to stay in power without direct election.

There were two arguments for the continuation of President dos Santos' stay in power during the post-Bicesse peace agreement. One is that after the 1992 elections, Angola was again in a state of war; therefore, if the president had stepped down, it would have left a power vacuum and made it easy for Jonas Savimbi, the leader of UNITA, to gain power by force. The second argument is that given the strong dominance President dos Santos had over the MPLA, the Angolan army, and the government, no one had the courage to question the validity of his mandate during the post-Bicesse wave. Nonetheless, Savimbi's refusal to accept the 1992 election results boosted President dos Santos's justification of keeping power after the 1992 uncompleted presidential elections.

As Campos and Vines argue (2008), political power in Angola is highly centralized around the president, more than in many other African countries; the presidency's power is almost unchallenged. They emphasize that President dos Santos is an extremely skilled operator of patronage networks. This generates bureaucratic instability; officials' power bases are temporary and insecure. President dos Santos controls alternative power centers that bypass traditional state structures. Alternative tools (such as oil-backed loans) are used to get things done but can damage institutional coherence. This makes it difficult for the government to set effective policies to fight poverty. As evidence, the results in Chapter III show there is widespread poverty, even more so now than during the time of war. Accordingly, the following section analyses the electoral process in Angola in order to further appreciate how the impasse in the legitimacy of state ruling parties and state leaders affects human development.

5.2. Ambiguity of Electoral Process

Multiparty competition is useful for democracy and human development. Without regular, free, and fair elections, it would be quite impossible to talk about good governance. Elections contribute to the building of trust and good governance by allowing for direct participation (Sen 1999). In a democratic society, political parties and elites need to gain people's political trust to win elections.[90] Having found that the condition of basic human rights in Angola is deteriorating, one could ask how the MPLA managed to win the 2008 elections by such a large margin. What strategies did the MPLA and its president take to regain people's trust in order to maintain power?

Theoretically, failing to promote and improve social services can be one of the major reasons for people's distrust of governments or political leaders (UNDP 2007). The preceding chapters demonstrated the extent to which the Angolan government is not doing enough to transform the country's rapid economic growth into creating jobs, providing access to education, and delivering services in an easy and transparent manner. Considering its poor delivery of social services, one could predict that that the MPLA could suffer a heavy defeat in the legislative elections if these are free and fair. Is the MPLA and its leadership aware of the underperformance of their government? Are they ready to accept criticisms of their deficiency to promote and protect of democratic human rights? Are they willing to improve social services in order to regain people's democratic trust?

Paradoxically, the degree of social satisfaction or dissatisfaction was not a firm indicator for the September 2008 legislative elections, the country's first elections in sixteen years. The MPLA won the elections with about 82 percent of the vote, followed by UNITA with

10 percent. The rest of the votes were divided among a dozen other parties and coalitions.

While African Union monitors said that the vote was "free and fair,"[91] the European Union's election observer mission found that Angola's elections fell short of international standards because the state-controlled radio, television, and daily newspaper were biased in favor of the government and because of flaws in some election procedures. Voter lists were distributed too late to be posted in most voting stations, making it impossible to check who had voted, though the use of indelible ink on voters' fingers helped guard against double voting (European Union 2008).

There were also prevalent delays in the opening of many polling places in Luanda and a failure to deliver sufficient ballots to them. The election authorities also did not accredit hundreds of trained election observers in Luanda, the mission said. Nonetheless, the European Union's report affirmed that the elections were peaceful and showed the Angolan people's "clear commitment to the country's democratic process and desire to leave behind a past marked by decades of war and civil conflict."[92] However, the MPLA's margin of victory leaves UNITA and other oppositions parties even more marginalized, a situation that some analysts worry could weaken the much-needed development of an effective political opposition.

Somehow, the 2008 election reinforced MPLA's dominance. As it won the two-thirds majority, 191 out of 220 seats, the MPLA has power to make sweeping changes to the constitution. The public money each party receives is based on its number of Parliament seats, and the opposition will have fewer now. Even with this election win, the MPLA's governing elite will still be trapped with a reputation for self-dealing and corruption, which shows up in studies by international organizations such as Transparency International and the World Bank Institute.[93]

The 2008 legislative election is similar to what happens in many African countries where dominant ruling parties find ways and means to win elections. Although scholars such Diamond and Plattner argue that the introduction of multiparty systems in post-Cold War Africa is a key pro-democratic innovation, others consider multiparty elections in many African countries just a façade of a democratic system, as in reality they do not help to consolidate the process of democratic governance.

In terms of the number of multiparty elections, the African continent has produced tremendous process. According to the international IDEA voter turnout, the level of political participation has increased in many African countries (IDEA 2006).[94] However, there has been a widespread argument that despite the majority of African countries having organized multiparty elections, there has been no notable change in governments (Bratton and van de Walle 1998).

Opposition parties in Angola and in many other African countries are finding it difficult to challenge dominant ruling parties. The reasons may be as Carothers (2002) argues—that the new generation of political parties in Africa is often characterized by weak organization, low levels of institutionalization, and inadequate links to the society that they profess to represent, especially in the rural communities. Hence, the idea that the introduction of multiparty systems in Africa will promote and sustain democracy is misleading. This is because a growing number of ruling dominant parties and leaders have impeded democratization processes on the continent (Manning 2005).

The permanence of one party in power can make a country different from others. It gives the ruling party "a continuous opportunity to pursue its historical agenda—shape its own following" (Panebianco 1988). The party can reshape the entire political profile of the country: symbols, values, and public expectation (Pempel 1990), and the dominant party's view becomes the consensus of the whole society (Giliomee and Simkins 1999). The MPLA, in power since 1975, was expected to at least retain its majority of 129 seats in the 220-member parliament, but winning more than two thirds gives it a free hand to be able to change the constitution in ways that could further entrench its dominance.[95] As a result, in 2010 the Angolan constitution was changed, introducing a parliamentary electoral system, thereby annulling presidential elections that should take place the same year.

Angolan President Jose Eduardo dos Santos, in power for thirty-two years, described the change to abolish direct presidential elections as a significant advance in the creation of the conditions for

116

a harmonious and sustainable country as well as consolidation of the country's democratic process. On the contrary, the new constitution is a consolidation of presidential power and a way for long-term political volatility. Soon after approval of the constitution in January 21, 2010; President dos Santos reshuffled his cabinet, a move seen as further consolidation of power. Angola is thus, since 2010, moving backward in the process of democratization.

The wiping out of presidential elections in the Angolan Constitution and considering the weakness of opposition parties in Angola signifies the MPLA president can hold in power as long as he want. Parliament in itself does not have that much power, under Article 66 of the Angolan Constitution; the president has the right to veto any new legislation that is approved by parliament. He is the commander in chief of the armed forces and also appoints ministers and judges of the Supreme Court.

Despite accusations that government officials in Angola have turned a blind eye to corruption and glaring social ills, President Jose dos Santos, in power for thirty-two years, is banking that voters will give the government credit for presiding over the country's economic boom. However, opposition parties (mainly UNITA) are attaching their hopes on discontent over the government's failure to improve widespread poverty and high unemployment.

There is empirical evidence that state leaders in the majority of countries ruled by dominant parties find it easier to win elections (Baker 1999). Literature on African politics shows that dominant state leaders in Africa do not care whether or not the people have trust on their governments. These leaders are mainly interested in having and keeping power by using any means. There are different means that dominant leaders use to dismiss their people's genuine will in elections and impose themselves in power. In many instances, they manipulate the electoral process and steal votes when needed.

While elite members of the government and the MPLA consider President dos Santos an extraordinary person, the view of the majority of Angolan citizens interviewed is completely different. Informal conversations with Angolans and expatriates revealed that there is widespread disappointment with the way the MPLA's presidency governs the country. Critics argue that the lack of people's trust in the MPLA's presidency of the country was a major stimulus for the parliament to modify the constitution and annul presidential elections.

Critics argue that the Angolan president takes advantage of the constitutional power he has to manipulate political agenda (IRIN 2006). Apart from the holding of legislative elections, Angola organized another major event, the football African Cup of Nations (CAF) in 2010. There was no doubt that financially Angola could organize such an event, as the country is potentially rich, with huge oil reserves (Simao 2005). In addition, there was hope that organizing the CAF would have some short- and long-term benefits for Angola (such as promoting tourism). However, the paradox is that Angola still has huge socioeconomic problems that need urgent solutions. The country is far from achieving the millennium development goals.

Hence, one would argue that if the government had enough money to handle the 2010 CAF, it should start by investing in social infrastructures, such as building schools and hospitals for the Angolan people in need before investing one-off in leisure events. But it came out clearly that the organization of CAN in Angola was useful tool for MPLA and its leadership to further manipulate the political situation in the country, as it was during that time the vote for charge of the national constitution passed to give unchallenged power to the ruling president. The question is how seriously committed the MPLA under the current presidency is to the democratic principle of good governance capable of sustaining human development.

5.3. Democratic Impasse in the Post-Luena Wave

This subsection analyses responses of research participants to four thematic questions represented in table 5.1, questions related to political factors affecting human development in Angola.[96] It is a continuation of data analyzed in the Chapter II. The first thematic question was to find how people rate their well-being in post-conflict Angola.

Table 5.1 General question over post-2002 HD in Angola* Origin Crosstabulation

Questions/Response categories	Respondents			Total
	Coastal	Countryside	Expatriate	
Q1 living condition is improving	10	5	4	19
living condition is not improving	24	28	12	64
living condition is worsening	20	13	-	33
Total	**54**	**46**	**16**	**116**
Q2 Democracy is not consolidating	29	31	15	75
Democracy is consolidating	17	3	-	21
n/a	8	12	1	20
Total	**54**	**46**	**16**	**116**
Q3 MPLA dominance	23	19	8	50
President dominance	17	16	8	41
Natural resources	14	11	-	25
Total	**54**	**46**	**16**	**116**
Q4 Democratisation of the MPLA	29	25	6	60
Change of state leadership	17	13	10	40
Good management of the natural resources	8	8	-	16
Total	**54**	**46**	**16**	**116**

Q1: How do you rate the quality of life in post-conflict Angola * Origin

Q2: What is your opinion about the process of democratisation in Angola? * Origin

Q3: What is your opinion of the main obstacles to democratisation in Angola? * Origin

Q4: What in your opinion can secure democracy in Angola? * Origin

The end of conflict in Angola had permitted some analysts, policy makers, donors, non-governmental organizations, and humanitarian agencies to predict the beginning of efforts to improve living conditions. However, the opinion of research participants was almost contradictory. Of the 116 respondents, only 19 said that the living conditions are improving. More than half of respondents said living conditions are not improving, and about 30 percent went as far as to state that living conditions are actually worsening. Why are the majority of respondents hopeless about their living conditions in the post-conflict Angola? In order to answer this question, it is important to conduct causal analysis.

The marginal distribution in the "living conditions are improving" column shows that ten of the nineteen respondents are from coastal regions. The conditional distribution of the countryside column demonstrates that most of its respondents considered that the condition of life is either not improving or worsening. Generally the living conditions of people living in the coastal region, where many of the country' major cities are situated, has always been relatively better than those located in the countryside (Minter 2002). This separation dates back to the colonial era, and it is described as regional and structural rather than ethnic in character. Furthermore, the war left widespread insecurity in the countryside. This is because UNITA' s military tactic was to make Angola ungovernable as their forces systematically targeted civilians and cut the economic links between city and countryside (Minter 2002).

As discussed in the Chapter II, despite the death of Savimbi and the signing of the 2002 cease-fire, Angolan people (mainly in the countryside) are still living in deplorable conditions. During my fieldwork in 2005, I had a group discussion in the countryside town of Luena, in the province of Moxico. The majority of participants insisted that their living conditions were far better during the time of war than at that time. This is because during the war, there were different humanitarian organizations providing food and health care. After the war, most of those organizations pulled out and left the responsibility of protection in the hands of the Angolan government. Members of the opposition accuse the MPLA government of using the large income from Angola's oil boom to feed the coastal region, chiefly Luanda, leaving the countryside neglected.[97]

The second thematic question was to find out what direction democratization in the post-conflict era was taking. Most of research participants equated democracy with a multiparty system and democratization with poverty reduction. Therefore, democratization should go together with the process of building credible and durable state institutions capable of promoting the well-being of people.

The majority of respondents were pessimistic rather than optimistic about the process of democratization in Angola. Most respondents considered that the process of democratization in Angola was failing. On the one hand, some research participants described democracy in Angola as an absence of war—a negative peace (Galtung 1996). For example, Maria[98] told me that during the time of war, a majority of Angolan women had to raise their children alone while their husbands were at war. "Democracy has came, there is no war . . . we can share responsibilities with our husbands," she said.

On the other hand, some of the respondents were very disappointed in the way Angola has been governed. On many occasions the Angolan ordinary people used the expression "thank God" (graça à Deus) when responding to a greeting. Ricardo,[99] a former combatant, gave his actual meaning of the imperative "thank God." He said, "Angolan people use this expression not because they are very religious but as a way to express their despair—the uncertainty about tomorrow. After the end of war, Angolans hoped that their life would change—the government would be accountable and responsible—but this is not the case." He added that the lack of democratic governance destroys the hope of many Angolan people.[100]

The resonance of this response led to the third thematic question, which analyzes why democratization is failing in Angola. As shown in the table 5.1, while about 22 percent of respondents considered that Angolan natural resources are the main cause of the stagnation of democratization in Angola, the majority deplored the dominance of the MPLA and its leadership as the major challenge to democracy in Angola.

As discussed in the preceding chapter, prior to 2002, Angola's natural resources were used to finance war and destroy the well-being of ordinary Angolan people. Many still worry that rather than promoting human development, the boom of natural resources, mainly oil and diamond revenues, would continue to consolidate the power of ruling elites and impede democratic principles and institutions in the post-conflict era (Hodges 2004).

There is a correlation between the findings represented in Table 5.1 and the conclusions of the Chapter II. Sustaining human development in Angola does not depend on the abundance of natural resources but on the way the ruling party and its leadership guides the country. Development and political literature show that the desire to stay longer in power that negatively affects human development is the common denominator of dominant parties and their leaders (Babu 2000; Houngnikpo and Kyambalesa 2001; Heidhues 2004). However, the strategies for control of political power by these leaders may differ from one country to another or from a period of time to another (Meredith 2005). Accordingly, the following are strategies used by the MPLA's leader to hold onto power.

Non-Compliance with Legal Regulations

As discussed in Chapter II, the Angolan National Constitution includes some regulations favorable to democratic principles. Furthermore, the country is a member of binding international treaties that encourage the practice of democracy. However, one could argue that the major problem is the fact that the Angolan government observes many laws that are not prejudicial to a president's power. Other regulations that support the promotion of fundamental freedoms and the well-being of people are largely violated (AI Report 2004; HRW 2006).

The major weakness of the current Angolan constitution is section one, which stipulates the duties and responsibilities of the president of the republic.[101] The majority of members of oppositions parties interviewed during my fieldwork said that the Angolan constitution provides the president with enormous power, which he abuses.

One of the top ministers of the Angolan government proudly declared that the actual president in power is an exceptional personality in Angola. "We put all the powers in his hands because he is the only one who can lead Angola,"[102] he said. This statement can be considered indicative of a cult, as one can argue that the majority of Angolan ministers are too busy pleasing and praising the president than to deliver services to people they are supposed to represent.

Often the MPLA regime misuses and deforms the constitutional law. A member of UNITA said that "the Angolan president uses his unlimited constitutional power to boycott democratic processes and oppress members of opposition parties."[103] For example five top elites of the MPLA government brought charges of defamation against the private weekly *Seminário Angolense* and its editor, Felizberto Graça Campos, in connection with the article that claimed to list Angola's richest men (Angolense 2004). The charges invoked Article 43 of the Press Law, which concerns "abuse of the press," and Article 407 of the Penal Code. HRW reports identify different incidences where members of the MPLA government oppressed opposition and critics voices (HRW 2004).

Member of opposition parties and civil society argue that in order to consolidate the process of democratization in Angola, government officials must observe the laws of the country. Furthermore, there is the need to review the current constitution and make it much more democratic. However, if the MPLA continue to occupy more than two-thirds of the seats in the National Assembly, it will be able to draft a constitution that suits its vision and most importantly that favors the president of the republic.

Corruption and Clientelism

The scale of Angola's corruption problem has been critically explored by some eminent organizations and scholars.[104] Many of my research participants used the following two Portuguese metaphoric expressions to describe corruption in Angola: Gasosa (soft drink) to describe palm greasing. This includes bribes give to police office, teachers or other civil servants. The other is gatuno (thief) to describe misuse of state wealth and a hijacking of state revenue into private bank accounts of members of the president's oligarchy.

While the gazosa phenomenon is a part of daily life that refers to bribes, the gatuno phenomenon involves big businesses. Although the Angolan government's initial efforts to improve transparency in the management of oil revenue are encouraging, the government's tediousness continues to hinder assessment of the management of public funds, contributing to the perception of persistent corruption (Hanson 2008).

Moreover, privileged by large revenues from the oil boom, Angola no longer depends largely on foreign aid or the donations of international financial institutions such as the World Bank and the International Monetary Fund (IMF). As a result, Angola is not obliged to follow the reforms and policy recommendations of such groups. However, critics argue that this invulnerability to pressure has fostered an opaque financial system rife with corruption, and has also destabilized democratic institutions.[105]

Experts and scholars argue that because power in Angola is concentrated around the president, he heads a patronage system that operates outside normal state channels (Hanson 2008). As a result, ad hoc commissions or other bodies that combine members of different government ministries tend to undermine the efficacy of formal institutions. Often these bodies operate in non-transparent manner (Shaxson, Neves, and Pacheco 2008). Moreover, members of opposition parties, civil society, and independent media accuse the president of giving business concessions to key political figures and Military Generals as a way to buy their supports (A Capital 2004). The work by Hodges presents a critical academic debate about the practices and causes of corruption in Angola (Hodges 2004).

Since the end of the civil war in 2002, the MPLA government has made some efforts to promote transparency. In conjunction with the World Bank, it established a program to monitor the majority of government expenditures as they occur. The ministry of finance publishes information on its website[106] about budgets, oil revenue, and Chinese financing with "an unprecedented level of detail," according to a May 2008 report from the Economist Intelligence Unit.[107] However, these efforts have attracted little attention outside Angola; many scholars, donors, and policymakers continue to perceive the country as highly corrupt. Some experts say the Angolan government hasn't helped to dispel this impression (Mai and Wisner 2007). A 2007 report on Angola from Council on Foreign Relations' (CFR) Centre for Preventive Action[108] notes that the Angolan government's answer to allegations of corruption is a combination of candor, denials, and evasion that is not always helpful and increases the skepticism with which many view Angola's current efforts (Mai and Wisner 2007).

However, a range of stakeholders in Angola report that the government has taken steps to improve transparency. In addition to signing the UN Convention against Corruption[109] and the AU Convention on Preventing and Combating Corruption,[110] Angola has established, with the World Bank, a program that monitors most government expenditures as they arise, and intends to monitor all expenditures by 2008. Furthermore, the situation of openness has improved in recent years with allegations of corruption and mismanagement broached openly in the Angolan media, everyday conversations, and public meetings. Nonetheless, the clearest test of Angola's commitment to transparency is whether it will fully participate in the Extractive Industries Transparency Initiative (EITI).[111]

Angola has taken some steps to meet EITI goals by publicizing its oil revenue on the Internet (by block and revenue type) and disclosing signing bonuses in the latest request round of offshore oil-block bidding. But Angola has yet to meet all EITI goals and continues to relinquish full participation.[112] By fully implementing EITI criteria, Angola could send a positive signal of its commitment to transparency that would influence foreign governments, the IMF, and the global private sector, thereby attracting more international investment capable of sustaining the human development that is so needed.

However, the Angolan government has avoided implementing measures that would erode the president's grip on power. According to the IMF report, measures to promote transparency have not extended to Sonangol. Angola continues to rank near the bottom of Transparency International's Corruption Perceptions Index; it is 168 of 179 countries in the 2010 ranking.[113] Unless Angola seriously fights corruption and restores transparency, it will always be difficult to translate its economic growth into sustainable human development.

Political Intimidation

Political intimidation is a harmful element of governance, as it negatively affects the quality of democracy and human development. A climate of political intimidation can make it difficult to promote basic human rights. It obstructs the capability and empowerment of citizens, thereby impeding sustainable human development. As discussed in Chapter II, members of opposition parties, civil society, and independent media investigated during my fieldwork in Angola accused the MPLA government of using political intimidation to silence opposition voices or critics. This argument is supported by international human rights organization such the Amnesty International and the HRW.

Political intimidation inhibits a democratic functioning of the electoral process, the media, and the party system. Human Rights organizations considered intimidation of opposition parties and the media ahead of parliamentary elections in Angola, as well as interference in the electoral commission, a threat to prospects for a free and fair vote in September 2008 (HRW 2008).

The finding of HRW's research mission conducted between March and June 2008 in provinces of Luanda, Huambo, Bie, Cabinda, and Benguela, shows that the Angolan government failed to fully ensure the right to free elections, and other rights critical to a fair poll, including the freedoms of expression and of assembly. The report said that the Angolan government is failing to fully meet basic duties set out in the Principles and Guidelines Governing Democratic Elections of the Southern Africa Development Community (SADC), of which Angola is a member.

Major areas of concern included the government's obligations to safeguard freedom of association and expression and access to the media by all stakeholders, and to establish an impartial national electoral body. The government did not do enough to provide adequate security to political parties participating in elections and to ensure political tolerance and full participation of citizens (HRW 2008).

Accordingly, political intimidation has played a major role in weakening opposition parties and spreading the MPLA's message to wider Angolans. In spite of the fact that the MPLA government affirmed that the elections would take place in an environment free of violence, a human rights organization documented numerous incidents of political violence involving the MPLA supporters through the voter registration period between November 2006 and May 2008 (HRW 2008). Political violence has occurred mainly in rural areas that were most affected by the civil war. Patterns of violence include periodic assaults by local MPLA supporters, sometimes involving traditional authorities and local MPLA leaders, against local UNITA party members and their property and party symbols (AI 2008).

Private media that could otherwise vehicle messages of opposition parties to the people are also highly intimidated. Amnesty International found clear indications that the media environment in Angola was highly restricted. In May 2008, the state television broadcaster suspended and took disciplinary action against presenter Ernesto Bartolomeu for supposed breach of professional confidences. Bartolomeu's "offense" was to admit publicly the degree of MPLA interference in the network's editorial policy. Moreover, opposition parties and viewpoints do not have the same access to media as the MPLA does. In July 2008, the government closed Radio Despertar, which according to Amnesty international was one of the few Angolan media outlets giving airtime to opposition political views.

Courts accelerated legal proceedings in pending criminal libel prosecutions against private media journalists prior to the September 2008 elections. In June 2008, a court sentenced Felisberto Graça Campos to a six-month prison sentence and ordered him to pay US$90,000 in damages following his conviction in three separate libel cases filed by government officials, which were pending for years. In June 2008, William Tonet (the editor of the private weekly *Folha 8*), also was to face trial in a libel case filed in 2004 by Ana Paula dos Santos, the president's wife, but the trial was postponed.

Observers accused the National Electoral Commission, whose mission is to ensure fairness, freedom, and transparency in the electoral process and to take positions that strengthen public trust in its role, of complying with orders from the MPLA (AI 2008).

In some cases, political intimidation in Angola was fatal. For example on November 11, 2004, Vincente Tembo, a UNITA deputy, was shot but not killed in a suburb of Luanda. Opposition groups claimed the shooting was politically motivated; however, the police denied this claim.[114] The most shocking incident was the death of Dr. Mfulumpinga Landu Victor, leader of the Democratic Party for Congress (PDP-ANA), shot dead by three unidentified men on July 2, 2004. While the government and police considered the killing a failed carjacking, some members of opposition parties and civil society, as well as ordinary citizens, believed the crime to be politically motivated (Angolense 2004).

In his article in the private weekly newspaper *Angolense*, Gilberto Neto argued that Dr. Mfulupinga was a genuine opponent of the MPLA (Neto 2007); he was the voice of Angola people. Hence, his brutal killing hugely disappointed ordinary Angolan people. "The death of Mfulumpinga means Angolan people no longer has a lawyer," said Ricardo.[115] Dr. Mfulumpinga was one of fervent democratic players in post-conflict Angola, one of the defenders of people basic rights. His assassination proves the extent to which there is still a lack of democratic values and culture of tolerance in Angolan politics. Furthermore, the brutal killing of Dr. Mfulumpinga created huge panic in opposition parties and weakened their role, as their leaders are very worried about their personal security due to secret political aggression. As a result, the MPLA found an opportunity to further establish its dominance.

The fourth thematic question in the questionnaire surveys was to find out what strategies were needed for consolidating democracy in post-conflict Angola. The majority of respondents argue that the MPLA should be democratized and there should be rotation of state leadership for democracy in Angola to consolidate. These issues were already discussed in the preceding sections. As discussed earlier, the change or rotation of personnel in the position of state leadership is healthy for the promotion and consolidation of democratic practices. Scholars, independent media, members of opposition parties, and civil society have all criticized the longevity of President dos Santos and his MPLA in power. They deplore the extent to which President dos Santos always finds ways to escape pressure and reinforce his authority through corruption, clientelism, oppression, and non-compliance with the national constitution (McMilan 2005).

5.4. What Is Next for the MPLA

As the party that has ruled Angola since its independence in 1975, the MPLA had a major influence in building and sustaining human development. Political parties can play critical roles to enable Sen's capability approach and UNDP's rights-based approach to human development. Political parties define and express people's needs and interests in a way that the public and political system can understand. A ruling political party that observes democratic principles and its internal democracy is likely to deliver services capable of promoting sustainable development.

However, ruling parties have controversial influence in many African countries. The rise of dominant party systems poses huge challenges to the idea of sustaining democracy and human development. This is because, in many cases, dominant leaders use their ruling dominant parties as personal tools to justify their façade of legitimacy (Bogaards 2004).

Through the process of consolidating its political supremacy, the MPLA managed to overcome internal revolts and UNITA's rebellion as well as adjust its ideology in order to attract international support. After independence, it embraced the Marxist Leninist bloc and ruled the country as a single party. Like many other African countries, the MPLA became a dominant party following the end of the Cold War. Despite the fact civil war ended in 2002, the MPLA has been criticized for paying lip service to the process of sustaining human development in the country.

Having won the majority in the National Assembly, the MPLA has the monopoly to form the government and pass resolutions with or without the support of opposition parties. The worry is, as discussed in the preceding chapters, the record of MPLA in promoting human development is poor. The long civil war was a major cause for the government incapacity to deliver services and sustain development prior to 2002. War is often very expensive, and there is no country in the world that builds a sustainable human development while fighting a violent war at home. Therefore, it is justifiable that the war played a major role in creating widespread poverty in post-colonial Angola.

However, despite the war in Angola ending more than nine years ago and even though the economy of the country is dramatically growing, the living conditions of the majority of the Angolan people are not improving. Activists, scholars, and members of the international community blame the MPLA's desire to hold onto power using unlawful means, such as corruption, for the government's inability to deliver services and protect the basic rights of people in post-conflict Angola (Minter 2002). What would prompt the MPLA to change its governance in the post-2008 elections? Why might the MPLA use its dominance in the National Assembly to make policies capable of sustaining human development in Angola? These questions can be answered through a comparative study with selected African countries governed by a dominant party system.

Although dominant parties have largely contributed to aggravating poverty in many African countries, in some countries dominant parties play major roles in sustaining human development. To support this argument, I have decided to briefly compare the case of Angola with three countries of the SADC region ruled by dominant. These countries are: Botswana, South Africa, and Zimbabwe. As shown in table 5.2, I compared selected economic and political factors to find out why some dominant ruling parties sustain human development while others do not.

Table 5.2 Illustrative Comparative Selected Variables of Human Development

Countries	Economical Factors (2007)			Political Factors (2007)		CPI		Outcomes HDI 2007	
	GDP per capita PPP ($)	GDP Growth (%)	IRCP %	PR Score	CL Score	Score	Rank	Value	Category
Angola	5,600	21.10	13.20	6	5	2.2	162	0.446	Low
Botswana	16,400	5.50	11.40	2	2	5.4	124	0.654	Medium
South Africa	9,800	5.10	5.00	2	2	5.1	121	0.674	Medium
Zimbabwe	200	- 6.10	976.40	7	6	2.1	151	0.513	Medium

CL: Civil Liberty – CPI: Corruption Perceptions Index – IRCP: Inflation rate(consumer prices) – PR: Political Rights – WBIG: World Bank Income Group

Sources: IMF, Transparency International, UNDP, the World Bank, World Audit

Compiled by the Author

The combination of dominant ruling party and dominant leaders makes it difficult for the country to sustain human development. For the sake of controlling and keeping power, dominant parties and their leaders can let down the economic development of their countries. For example, in Zimbabwe, for ten years after President Robert Gabriel Mugabe came into power, he managed to improve the social-economic condition of citizens. However, since he began his land redistribution program, the socioeconomic situation of Zimbabweans has dramatically dropped[116] (*The Economist* 2005).

The major difference between countries ruled by dominant parties and non-dominant parties is often political. Countries ruled simultaneously by dominant party systems and dominant state leaders often have poor scoring or rank of political factors. In these countries, dominant leaders use their dominant parties as a personal tool for justifying their façade of legitimacy. For example, Robert Mugabe controls the direction of ZANU-PF (Zimbabwe African National Union – Patriotic Front). There is a strong belief within his party that should Mugabe step down, the party, the state, and the nation will crumble (Sachikonye 2002). Similarly, MPLA's partisans believe that President dos Santos is irreplaceable at the leadership of Angola.

Attempting to control political power, dominant leaders damage the reputation of their people and nations. For example, while in 2008 Botswana had witnessed another smooth transition of power,[117] President Robert Mugabe in Zimbabwe, who has already served twenty-eight years in Zimbabwe, refused to give up power and got another term in office. President Mugabe, like dos Santos in Angola and other many dominant leaders in Africa are seen as symbols of the liberation struggle within their parties; they have been able to use their parties' unchallengeable liberation credential ideals and connect them with the electorate during elections. Thus, to justify their stay in power, they often refer the foundational myths of their parties or the role they played historically (Mozaffar 2005, Diamond and Plattner 1999).

As data in Table 5.2 describes, the scores of political rights[118] and civil liberties[119] of both Angola and Zimbabwe are high. Moreover, their scores in Transparency International (TI)'s Corruption Perceptions Index (CPI) are lower.[120] In these circumstances it is difficult for people to participate in the decision-making process, enjoy their fundamental human rights, and hold government officials accountable. When a country is highly corrupted, it is likely that its political leaders will not be vertically and horizontally accountable. As these leaders are dominant, citizens are often afraid to challenge them even when they are misusing public revenues in their private businesses and failing to implement policies capable of sustaining human development.

The condition of a country's human development can be partially affected by economic and political factors of the past. For example, though the Zimbabwean economy is now one of the worst in Africa, its HDI's rank is still higher than Angola with one of the world's fastest GDP growth rates. This is because compared to Angola, Zimbabwe at the time of independence was well developed and during the ten years after colonization, Zanu-PF's government had successfully sustained economic development. Accordingly, poor human development in post-conflict Angola is partially a result of legacies of the past. The post-independence civil war, Cold War geopolitics, and single party control and dictatorship had not helped Angola to build a socioeconomic infrastructure capable of sustaining human development.

It is true Angola needs time to rebuild the country, which experienced widespread destruction during decades of conflicts.[121] No one expects Angola to change its HDI radically just in this short period following the 2002 cease-fire. However, as discussed in the preceding chapters, the gap between the GDP growth and HDI is so big. With its rapid economic growth, Angola should at least be able to start slightly improving its HDI. Failing to do so symbolizes bad governance. Thus, if the government does not improve its human rights and corruption records, it will be hard to sustain human development.

Botswana and South Africa represent one of good examples whereby dominant ruling parties can sustain human development. The governing parties: Botswana Democratic Party (BDP)[122] in Botswana and the African National Congress (ANC) play a major role in improving health, education, and creating jobs in their respective countries. Since 1994, Botswana and South Africa have scored above 0.600 on UNDP's human development index. Contrary to some African countries where dominant parties function as private institutions of dominant leaders, in Botswana and South Africa, dominant parties elaborate democratic policies able to sustain human development.

Arguably, the dominant parties in Botswana and South Africa stay in power because opposition parties are struggling to find impressive electoral programs to attract voters. One can assert that for cases like that of South Africa, the main opposition parties, the Democratic Alliance (DA) or the Inkatha Freedom Party (IFP), would find it difficult to challenge ANC in power. This is because the ANC may still be considered by the majority of South African people to be the party of unity and reconciliation. Most importantly, the ANC is the party of Nelson Mandela who is considered the father of freedom of South Africans and an exceptional example of good leadership in Africa. Therefore, the majority of South African people might prefer to put their trust in the ANC than on other political parties.

The role of state leaders has major impact on the outcomes of human development. It is very difficult to sustain human development in countries where state leaders do not observe democratic principles and rule of internal democracy of parties (Baker 1998). What makes the difference in countries like Botswana and South Africa is the fact that no one (including the head of state) is above the law. State leaders in these countries abide by democratic regulations of their countries and political parties; they are accountable not only to the governmental hierarchy but also directly to people they represent.

Moreover, these leaders can be punished if they extrapolate democratic norms. For example, in September 2008, Mr. Thabo Mbeki formally resigned as president of South Africa, a day after accepting a call by the governing ANC to quit.[123] The pressure by members on the ANC on their own leader and President Mbeki's acceptance to step down is a good example of observance of democratic principles and party's internal rule of democracy. Therefore, this type of leadership can stimulate good governance.

As stated earlier, good governance is crucial to the sustainability of human development. As the data in Table 5.2 shows, both Botswana's and South Africa's governments have a good record of protecting political rights and civil liberties. Moreover, these governments are not heavily corrupted. Furthermore, the two countries have a good ranking of democracy in the World Audit.[124] Good political indicators combined with good economic factors make it possible for the BDP and the ANC governments to sustain human development in their respective countries.

The attempt to improve human development in Angola is at a crossroads. On the one hand, Angola resembles Botswana and South

Africa in that it has largely improved its economic policies, enabling the country to increase its GDP growth and reduce rates of inflation and foreign debt. On the other hand, Angola resembles Zimbabwe as the MPLA government is not doing enough to promote and protect basic human rights of people nor is it fighting widespread corruption and political intimidation that weaken opposition voices.

These political factors prevent Angola from having a fair and adequate redistribution of national revenues to all Angolans. Hence, the rapid economic growth in Angola can play a role in sustaining human development only if the MPLA adapts a good governance approach based on the respect human dignity of all Angolan, helping the poor, and more importantly observing O'Donnell's principle of vertical and horizontal accountability.

Summary

The chapter's main finding is that the combination of dominant ruling party and dominant state leadership is the main cause for poor human development in post-conflict Angola. The MPLA and its leadership dominance of the Angolan politics make it difficult for oppositions to function and campaign. The MPLA leadership has dominated its organizational structures and the government institutional hierarchy throughout the post-colonial era.

Its leader, President dos Santos, managed to stay in power following the uncompleted multiparty election in 1992 and justified his political image internationally. Since the end of war in 2002, the MPLA has been enlarging its international connections and has begun new relations with countries like China to consolidate its power. In addition, the fact that Angola has one of the worst rankings in the world on corruption perception, political rights, and civil liberties affects the government's capacity to transform the country's economic boom into sustainable human development. While social contract implies that legitimate power must be derived from the consent of the people, this was not often experienced in Angola. There are no clear mechanisms that allow Angolan people to withdraw their consent for MPLA's leadership. The September 2008 legislative election and the abolition of the direct presidential elections represents a critical juncture in post-conflict, as it reflects the fact that the MPLA and its leader will further dominate Angola for years that can bring the country back into violent conflicts or mass disorder as a result of people's frustration.

Theoretically, given the fact that the war in Angola is over, the social contract shall encompass the people's rights to freely delegate power to their representatives and the government's responsibilities to respond to people needs of human development. However, despite the new political innovations, the MPLA's traditional legacies may not change as it still acting as the liberation movement. It continues to oppress opposition voices and politically manipulate the economic situation for political reason. Although the MPLA claims full legitimacy after the victory of the 2008 elections, it is hard to see how responsive it is given the fact that it is the sole majoritarian party in the National Assembly.

As the MPLA occupies more than two-thirds of the seats in the National Assembly, it has the monopoly to pass legislation and to form the government. This will further contribute to the consolidation of non-accountable and non-responsible government. Therefore, sustaining human development in a post-conflict setting will largely depend on political influences of the MPLA. If the MPLA readjusts its internal democracy and its leadership obeys democratic principles, human development will improve rapidly. However, if it continues to maintain of the person-centered system of government, the fight against poverty in Angola will be hard and long regardless the country's economic performance.

VI. CONCLUSION AND
POLICY IMPLICATION

It was possible to understand through this book where Angola has gone, not gone, and still needs to go as measured by the Sen–UNDP criteria. The book presents proper employment of mixed data-driven analysis based on field surveys and qualitative/normative analysis. Moreover, it tells non-specialists in the region what is going on and also allows specialists on other African and Southern African countries to compare notes and critiques in a detailed and empirically supported way. There are complex answers to the problem addressed in the book, namely, that human development is not occurring in Angola despite economic growth having been enabled by the post-conflict Accords and oil money.

The post-conflict impasse is explained by the fact that, on the one hand, the country is experiencing a remarkable improvement of economic indicators, and, on the other hand, the majority of the population lives in extreme poverty. Angola is blessed with huge natural resources, such as diamonds, forests, oil, the sea, and so on, which present a potential for longstanding economic growth. The civil war, lasting for almost three decades after the independence of Angola in 1975, was one of the main causes of poor human development in Angola. The situation in Angola changed dramatically during 2002, when the MPLA and UNITA signed a comprehensive cease-fire agreement, the Luena Memorandum of Understanding, even though the policies and political choice of the ruling party did not do anyone any favors in the fight against poverty in post-conflict Angola.

To answer the question of whether or not the post-conflict economic boom contributes to sustainable human development in Angola, there are two opposing views. Optimists believe that Angola has, since the end of war, headed, and is still heading, in the right direction.

The critical assessment of macroeconomic indicators in Chapter III reaffirmed the extent to which economy in post-conflict Angola is booming. The national output in post-conflict Angola looks strong with a sharply increasing GDP, improvement in the inflation rate, and decrease in external debt. It would be, therefore, ungrateful not to give the Angolan government credit for generating such economic progress. Economic growth, an important factor in reducing poverty and generating the resources necessary for human development, would be further stimulated if the government's objective to boost the agriculture sector were realized.

Instead of being overwhelmed by praises of economy stabilization, the Angolan government must explore the room available for further improvement. For example, Angola is still ranked near the bottom of the World Bank's Doing Business Index. Moreover, in 2010, the World Bank ranked Angola among the most difficult places in the world to do business. Blooming business opportunities contribute to the creation of jobs, which, in turn, provide households with financial security to satisfy their basic needs and enjoy their fundamental human right to dignity. Therefore, the Angolan government must continue to work hard in order to find means and ways that can enable it to improve the business climate in post-conflict Angola.

Pessimists consider that Angola is missing opportunities due to the fact that despite rapid economic growth in the post-conflict era, people's living conditions remain poor. A critical analysis of the rights to health, education, and work, as well as freedoms of expression, association, and movement, demonstrates the extent to which the majority of Angolan people are still living in poor conditions. Although the Angolan government has launched various projects to rebuild social infrastructures, since the end of the civil war, their impact on the living conditions of the poor is not yet obvious. As a result, the government must be prepared to accept criticism from pessimists.

It is important to bear in mind that criticism is normal—no government in the world, regardless of its policies, can escape from it. There are both negative critics that aim to frustrate governments and positive or constructive critics that intend to contribute to the search of socioeconomic progress. Therefore, the government must be prepared to welcome any kind of criticism and defy those negative ones through government actions and programs, to capitalize on the positive ones to revise and improve government policies. Thus, this book raises a debate about what the Angolan government, international community, and research centers can do to boost the curve of human development in post-conflict Angola.

The state, the major player in promoting human development, is the only institution with sufficient legitimate power to guide people and protect their interests. However, it is important to bear in mind that during the almost twenty-seven years of war following independence, there was no favorable atmosphere for the Angolan government to sustain human development. Portuguese colonial legacy, civil war, Cold War geopolitics, and breaching of peace agreements were major factors that contributed to poverty exacerbation, and their hangover is obvious in the post-conflict era. Thus, improving people's living conditions in post-conflict Angola will take time and also the government must show some sort of willingness to change people's lives.

Of course, economic growth has much potential for sustaining human development in Angola. However, Angolan fiscal, budgetary, and development policies are crucial to realizing such potential. A replication of expanded oil production in Angola between 2001 and 2010 suggests that if there are good policies, oil revenues have the ability to significantly reduce poverty levels. To sustain human development, rather than simply promoting economic growth, government policies in Angola need to specifically target the poor and seek to reduce inequalities through income redistribution and the improvement of social services and infrastructures, as well as through stimulating the agricultural and industrial sectors.

Angola is one of important countries in southern and central Africa that, if stable, has the potential to not only improve the living conditions of its people but to contribute to socioeconomic development of the African continent and play a key role in collective efforts of securing international peace and security. Some countries have recently shown that they intend to consent to open bilateral cooperation with Angola. This is an encouraging step, if the due cooperation takes place under a principle of mutual respect and stimulates investments that can create more jobs for jobless Angolans.

Apart from developing policies for economic growth, sustaining human development in post-conflict Angola will require effective protection of fundamental human rights. There is no doubt that the conditions of basic freedoms of association, expression, and movement, following the civil war, have improved and are still improving. The liberalization of media and authorization of political parties and civil society organizations to operate provide some good examples of promotion of fundamental freedoms in post-conflict Angola. Nonetheless, despite some of the positive steps that have been taken, many more efforts are needed in order to consolidate institutions for the promotion of freedoms of association, expression, and movement in post-conflict Angola. For example, there is a need to improve regulations enabling an effective participation of women in the decision-making process and promoting the right to demonstration, which are important components of fundamental freedoms.

The promotion of economic, social, and cultural rights is necessary to meet basic human needs, such as food, water, housing, education, health care, and employment. Angola is one of the countries in the world with the lowest life expectancies. According to existing empirical date on health conditions in Angola, the major social indicators of the right to health, such as life expectancy, malnutrition, and access to water and sanitation, deteriorated generally during the war and are still alarming. The poor conditions of the right to health contribute to the deterioration of living conditions. Therefore, the country needs to use part of its national revenues rationally to boost the health system. A healthier population is better equipped to sustain economic growth and human development.

Issues of availability of jobs and equal treatment at work are challenging in post-conflict Angola. The country has a high unemployment rate, and the majority of the population is employed in informal markets. Finding suitable jobs has become more difficult even for the few skilled and qualified Angolans. As a result, households do not have the financial security to pay for their basic needs or taxes. Poor work conditions and salary levels hinder people's capability for self-determination. In order to attempt to create more jobs, the Angolan government should find ways and means to set up regulations to protect Angolan citizens during recruitment and at work. The government shall monitor all companies and international organizations and prohibit them from violating the fundamental right of work of Angolan people. Failure to comply with the right to work undermines the prospect of sustaining human development in post-conflict Angola, as people no longer possess the capacity and confidence to take responsibility for their own lives.

Angolans have never fully enjoyed their basic right to education. During colonial times, education was mostly limited to the white minority; after independence, the civil war posed a major challenge to the development of the educational system in Angola. The nature of the major problems concerning education in Angola entails both quantitative and qualitative aspects. There are a limited number of universities and research centers, the academic facilities are poor, and there is a small number of qualified lecturers, all of which affects the quality of the educational system in the country. Therefore, efforts are needed to improve the educational system in post-conflict Angola at all levels.

Angola needs to multiply the number of qualified human resources for its sustainable development. Although in some circumstances, expertise from expatriates is inevitably required, sustaining human development will face a huge challenge if Angola relies solely or largely on expatriates' expertise. Expatriates, whose wages are often extremely high, leave a vacuum when they return to their countries of origin, thereby posing a major challenge to socioeconomic development. Thus, training, valuing, and caring for highly skilled Angolans is one of the key strategies for sustaining human development in post-conflict Angola.

The process of sustaining human development in Angola requires accurate data collection and analysis at national, provincial, and municipal levels to explain the scale of poverty—it needs to examine the kind of policies and interventions that might boost people's living conditions. Members of Parliament shall not only stay in Luanda; on the contrary, they shall conduct regular consultations with people in their constituencies in order to find out about the real problems concerning the population and make recommendations on the policies that can improve their living conditions. Academic institutions such as universities shall create research centers to conduct in-depth analysis of poverty-related issues and make constructive policy recommendations.

The fundamental role the Angolan university has in the processes of building democratic institutions capable of transforming the country wealth into human development could arguably depend not only on the vested interests of staff and students, but also on their quantity and the quality of knowledge they produce. The position and reality of the university as a bridge between the state and civil society account for its uncertainty and dilemma in Angola. The intellectuals and the university as the mediator of knowledge, ignorance, or mediocrity have been at the center of power and powerlessness in the post-colonial era in Angola. The ambivalent position and importance of the university as an institution lies in its appeal both to the reactionary and revolutionary forces in society. Unfortunately, in Angola, the MPLA regime have co-opted intellectuals to provide the conceptual clamor they need to justify their stay in power, promote a culture of violence, silence progressive views, foster mediocrity, and promote clientelism and a cult of personality.

Therefore, it is crucial to first conduct a critical distinction in post-conflict Angola between intellectuals who are free from political and economic constraints, on the one hand, and those who are subjugated by party political affiliations and economic dependence of all kinds, on the other. Then we must seek to know to what extent survival politics has triumphed over genuine democratization in Angola, creating, in the process, a type of intellectual who seems more preoccupied by politics of increasing mobility than with theoretical activities and the pursuit of science and knowledge. We must also explore how the diminishing resources for universities and the loss in value of academic qualifications have bred or exacerbated opportunism, corruption, mediocrity, and politicization in academic circles in Angola. How do academics, who have, for one reason or another, abandoned their vanguard role in favor of vested political interests, justify their options?

Programs of structural adjustment and the unequal flows of labor, capital, and knowledge are reproduced within the Angolan academy and significantly mediated by the often self-serving and extractive MPLA government. Global economics, transnational disciplinary discourses, national welfare, state political programs, and the local universities and local social affiliations set up competing prospects within which intellectuals must establish orientations and affinities, often with a significant measure of ambivalence. While some Angolan intellectuals may be compelled (for various reasons including economic adversity and political repression) to pursue careers elsewhere, for those who remain within Angola, the question is one of how intellectual orientations are formed, how different interests are recognized and articulated, and what limitations are placed on the pursuit of these interests. Thus, it is crucial for the Angolan university and intellectuals to free themselves from the oppression, manipulation, and co-optation employed by the MPLA so that they can contribute toward building democratic institutions able to promote human development.

So far, despite imbalances caused by international financial crises and the fall in oil prices in world markets in 2008–9, the empirical data discussed in this book shows that the Angolan economic situation is doing rather well. The country needs to take this opportunity to develop social infrastructures capable of sustaining human development. However, it is a political choice that will determine whether Angola will transform its booming economy into sustainable human development. Hence, it would be useful for Angola to regularly assess its macroeconomic and people's basic needs, building a system for accountable public spending, constraining political patronage, building post-conflict unity, and growing the non-oil economy.

The negative outcomes of corruption and the resource curse are major challenges in the attempt to sustain human development in post-conflict Angola. The Angolan government will need to implement government reforms and increase transparency in order for Angola to take full advantage of its rich national resources. Moreover, the Angolan government needs to reform its economic policies: encouraging diversification of businesses as well as making basic social investments that are capable of empowering the poor, reducing inequalities through income redistribution, and improving social services and infrastructures, as well as stimulating the agricultural and industrial sectors.

The behavior of state leaders and the ruling parties has major implications on human development. One of the major change challenges in post-conflict Angola is the dominance of President dos Santos over the MPLA and over the Angolan government. Observers and analysts of President dos Santos ponder over whether Angola will experience a political perplexity or vacuum of power such as in the DRC after Mobutu Sese Seko or Cote d' Ivoire after Félix Houphouët-Boigny. It is crucial for Angolans (members of the ruling and opposition parties as well as civil society and academics) to prepare progressively for a democratic and peaceful transition of power to avoid any potential vacuums of power in the post-Santos era.

It would be very difficult to promote human development in Angola without an active political willingness of the MPLA and its leadership. As the dominant party, the impact of the MPLA on the decision-making process and living conditions in Angola is critical. Therefore, building democracy in Angola should not be limited to the symbolic stage of organizing multiparty elections but should be about crafting institutions capable of delivering services for the welfare system.

The Need for a Welfare Democracy in Angola

The discussion in this book clearly shows that a failure to promote human development in post-conflict Angola is no longer economically motivated but is politically motivated. Angola has enough wealth to improve the living conditions of its people but lack of good governance is a problem. Therefore, there is a need for a welfare democracy in post-conflict Angola that involves an attempt to maximize social justice through strategies of empowerment. Democratization in Angola should go hand in hand with the process of building credible and durable state institutions capable of promoting people's well-being.

There are two fundamental factors that can contribute to the consolidation of a welfare democracy. The first one is the need to promote non-dominant leadership. Dominant leaders are unlikely to steal votes, use force, corruption, and clientelism as a way to hold onto power. Therefore, many of my research participants argue that the dominance of the MPLA and its leadership makes it difficult for the Angolan government to deliver services capable of improving their living conditions.

As clearly explained, the core of Angola's problem lies in the undemocratic nature of the MPLA and not so much in that it is a dominant party. Certainly, Botswana's and South Africa's structures are similar as post-colonial forms of state, but the reason why their dynamic is different is yet uncertain. The Sen–UNDP synthesis says that this should be different and even predicts how human developmental outcomes would be different if it were. But this book explains why it is the way it is and gives a transformational strategy derived from the dialectics or chemistry of social change in Angola. Sen's discourse presumes a modicum of democracy that can be used to build more democracy and human capabilities. But the question is where to begin when hegemonic control is near total as in Angola.

Through the process of consolidating its political supremacy, the MPLA managed to overcome internal revolts and UNITA's rebellion as well as adjust its ideology in order to attract international support. It embraced the Marxist Leninist bloc after Angola's independence and ruled the country as a single party. Following the introduction of the multiparty system after the end of the Cold War, the MPLA rapidly transformed itself into a dominant party and continued to obstruct democratic political change. In spite of the end of the civil war in 2002, the MPLA continued to pay lip service to the process of democratization in Angola in order to maintain its dominance of power. Therefore, in order to have a genuine change in post-conflict Angola, the MPLA must change. It must undertake the process of building its internal democracy, and there should be effective competition within the party system. This process can be possible only through the internal reform of the MPLA and well-coordinated external pressure by opposition parties, civil society, and academicians, as well as by the Angolan people.

Another fundamental factor for building a welfare democracy is the consolidation of a democratic multiparty system. Democratic party system requires party competition, which is vital for a democratic system. Enhanced party competition is a crucial element of the democratization process, and some African countries are significantly more competitive than they were before the end of the Cold War. However, the rule of a dominant party system poses major challenges to a democratic multiparty system. Accordingly, in order to consolidate a democratic multiparty system, there should be effective competition within the party system. As argued in favor of the examples of Botswana and South Africa, the dominant party should observe party regulations and promote effective electoral competition.

The major difference between the dominance of the BDP in Botswana, the ANC in South Africa, and the MPLA in Angola lies in the role of state leadership as well as internal organization.

- While in Botswana and South Africa the dominant parties listen to people's demands and try to transform them into policies, in Angola, like in Zimbabwe, the dominant parties impose their will on people and oppress any opposition voice.
- While in Botswana and South Africa the dominant parties democratically determine the direction of their countries and their leaders obey the decisions of their parties, in Angola, like in Zimbabwe, the leaders of dominant parties impose their will on their parties and use them as tools to hold onto power.
- While in Botswana and South Africa the dominant parties and their leaders care about the dignity of people, in Angola, like in Zimbabwe, the dominant parties and their leaders care about power—they use propaganda and oppression to rule.
- While in Botswana and South Africa economic growth does not prevent the country from democratically changing state leadership, the non-development economic growth in post-conflict Angola is used to justify the extension of the president's time in power.

Thus, building welfare democracy does not require exclusion of the MPLA, but its radical internal democratic reform. The party must move from short-term vision to long-term; it must move from an individual-led party to an institution-led party. No one should be above the party; in fact, all members, regardless their positions, must comply with the direction of the party.

The recommendations in the preceding sections are logical in terms of the synthesis in this book, but how well can this analysis predict their implementation? Appeals to human rights observance in the Angolan constitution and treaties, naming and shaming by intergovernmental bodies, and democratic education at the grassroots level are good measures. But what about the independent power of the courts in Angola, in contrast to Botswana's and South Africa's? What can Angolans do to bring suit against their government in terms of human rights? What can they do to gain access to international government organizations and be able to travel freely within the country? What can think tanks and universities do to be credible for democratic education? What can they do to penetrate the grassroots units of the MPLA? Can the educational strategy transcend ethnic suspicions so that the MPLA does not interpret it as UNITA propaganda and so discredit it?

Of course, considering the current high level of complaisance, favoritism, political manipulation, cult of personality and oppression by the ruling party in Angola, it will not be easy to build institutions for welfare democracy. But progressive Angolans, both within and outside the MPLA, should not sit down and wait; rather, they should begin the struggle for democratic political change for a sustainable welfare democracy.

Apart from the two fundamental factors mentioned above, I have identified three complementary factors that are important in the promotion of a welfare democracy. First, there should be a fair and well-coordinated democratic assistance. Democratic assistance to Africa by the members of the international community is producing little effect (Burnell 2000). The international community poses two major problems to the idea of democratic assistance in Africa. The first problem is the fact that some members of the international community stand on the idea of supporting democracy in Africa yet give full support to undemocratic leaders who obstruct democratic processes (Southall 2003).

The second problem is the fact that in some African countries (such as Angola), there are too many international organizations working in the field of democratic assistance. Sometimes, these organizations duplicate their actions and lack any form of coordination, creating confusion within local stakeholders (Ndulo 2006). Thus, it is important to revisit the democratic assistance approach in order to make it fair and well-coordinated. Only then can democracy assistance enable the process of building a welfare democracy.

Second, building a welfare democracy calls for the need to explore issues related to the concept of "democratic education" (Gutmann 1987). Little has been written about issues of democratic education in Angola. The lack of public democratic education[125] is one of the major contributors to democratic stagnation and reversal in many African countries. In some countries, as explained in the case of Angola, discussion of issues related to democracy is a reserved domain for intellectual and political elites. Therefore, when people are not aware of democratic values and principles, politicians can easily manipulate them for selfish purposes.

Democratic education can empower citizens to make their leaders accountable and credible. Therefore, an appropriate methodology should be found in order to make democratic education in Angola open not only to specialized institutions (such as political parties and government agencies) but to all organizations in society, including schools and universities. Moreover, there is a need to find appropriate strategies for democratic education in Africa to include issues of ethnicity and cultural diversity.

Third, building a welfare democracy calls for the need to explore issues related to the political economy of democracy. Natural resources contribute to a number of Africa's burdens such as poverty, corruption, dictatorship, and war, which damage human development. The case study of Angola demonstrates the extent to which natural resources (mainly oil and diamonds) in Africa suffer from a bad reputation. Accordingly, an issue for further research would be to explore the extent to which democratizing state leaderships, party systems, and improving resource rent[126] can open an opportunity for promoting human development while promoting social inclusion and economic development, which are crucial for a welfare democracy. This would require us to find a methodological approach to avoid the resource curse theory in the context of democratization in Angola.

Even though the economic indicators in post-conflict Angola are impressive, there is much yet to be done in order to improve the political factors in Angola that influence human development. The fact that Angola has one of the worst ranking positions in the world concerning corruption perception, political rights, and civil liberties influences the government's ability to transform the country's economic boom into sustainable human development. Therefore, in order to promote human development in Angola, there is a need to reinforce horizontal and vertical accountability. The MPLA government has two choices to make: If it adopts Botswana's or South Africa's approach of party dominance, human development will sustain rapidly. However, if it sticks to Zimbabwe's type of party and state leadership dominance, the fight against poverty in Angola will be hard regardless of the country's economic performance.

ABBREVIATIONS AND ACRONYMS

AFD	African Development Bank
AGOA	Africa Growth and Opportunity Act
AI	Amnesty International
ANC	African National Congress
ANIP	Angola's National Agency for Private Investment
OECD	Organization for Economic Co-operation and Development
BDHRL	Bureau of Democracy Human Rights and Labour
BDP	Botswana Democratic Party
BMI	Business Monitor International.
BNA	Banco Nacional de Angola (Angolan National Bank)
BP	British Petroleum
BTI	Bertelsmann Transformation Index
CABGOC	Cabinda Gulf Oil Company
CAF	African Cup of Nations
CCPR	Covenant on Civil and Political Rights
CEDWA	Committee on the Elimination of Discrimination Against Women
CE.ne	China Economic Net
CESCR	Committee on Economic, Social and Cultural Rights
CFB	Benguela Railway
CFR	Council on Foreign Relations
CIDCM	Centre for International Development and Conflict Management
CIMPE	Comissão Interministrial para o Processo Eleitoral
CIRs	Centres of Revolutionary Instruction
CNE	National Electoral Commission
COMESA	Common Market for Eastern and Southern Africa
CONCP	Conference of Nationalist Organizations of the Portuguese Colonies

CPI	Corruption Perceptions Index
CPR	Civil and Political Rights
CSRC	China Securities Regulatory Commission
DA	Democratic Alliance
DDR	Disarmament, Demobilization and Reinsertion
EBA	Everything But Arms
EITI	Extractive Industries Transparency Initiative
EMRP	Emergency Multisector Recovery Program
Endiama	Empresa Nacional de Diamantes de Angola
EPA	Economic Partnership Agreement
ESCR	Economic, Social and Cultural Rights
EU	European Union
FAA	Forca Armada Angolana
FALA	Forças Armadas de Libertação de Angola
FAO	Food and Agriculture Organization of the united Nations
FAPLA	Popular Armed Forces for the Liberation of Angola
FESA	Eduardo Dos Santos Foundation
FNLA	National Front for the Liberation of Angola
FONGA	Forum das Organizações Não Governamentais de Angola
FRELIMO	Liberation Front of Mozambique
FRAIN	Revolutionary Front for the National Independence of the Portuguese Colonies
GDP	Gross Domestic Product
GNP	Gross National Product
GRN	Gabinete de Reconstrução Nacional
GSP	Generalised System of Preferences
HDI	Human Development Index
HRW	Human Rights Watch
GURN	Government of Unity and National Reconciliation
IDEA	International Institute for Democracy and Electoral Assistance
IDPS	Internally Displaced Persons
IDRS	International Development Research Centre
IEA	International Energy Agency
IFP	Inkatha Freedom Party
IMF	International Monetary Fund
IRI	International Republican Institute
IRIN	Integrated Regional Information Networks

JA	Journal de Angola
JMPLA	Juventude do MPLA
LIMA	League for Angolan Women
MONUA	United Nations Observer Mission in Angola
MPLA	Popular Movement for the Liberation of Angola
MSF	Medecins Sans Frontieres
MPR	Popular Movement of the Revolution
MUSA	Movement for Socialist Unity in Angola
NRM	National Resistance Movement
OHCHR	Office of the United Nations High Commissioner for Human Rights
OCED	Organization for Economic Co-operation and Development
OCHA	Office for the Coordination of Humanitarian Affairs
ODC	Civil Defence Organization
OMA	Organização da Mulher Angolana
PADEPA	Partido de Apoio Democrático e Progresso de Angola
PDP/ANA	Democratic Party for Congress
PCA	Angolan Communist Party
PCP	Portuguese Communist Party
PLUA	Party of the United Struggle for Africans in Angola
PAIGC	African Party for the Independence of Guinea and Cape Verde
PRS	Social Renewal Party
PSI	Policy Support Instrument
SADC	Southern African Development Community
TPA	Angolan Public Television
UNDP	United Nations Development Program
UNAVEM	United Nations Angola Verification Mission
UNITA	National Union for Total Independence of Angola
UNSC	United Nations Security Council
UDHR	Universal Declaration of Human Rights
UNICEF	United Nations Children's Fund
UNFPA	United Nations Population Fund
UNESCO	United Nations Educational, Scientific, and Cultural Organization
USGS	United States Geological Survey
UNTA	National Union of Angolan Workers
WHO	World Health Organization
WSSD	World Summit on Sustainable Development

ENDNOTES

1. Data gathered by international financial institutions, the International Monetary Fund (IMF) and the World Bank show that the Angolan gross domestic product (GDP) has been growing sharply and inflation and external debts have drastically decreased.
2. Sen 1999; UNDP 2000; Nyamu-Musembi and Cornwall 2004. The Capability Approach is a conceptual framework for evaluating social states in terms of human well-being. It encompasses functional capabilities or "substantial freedoms" (such as the ability to live longer, engage in economic activities, or participate in political life) and the substantive freedoms, which enable people to access to resources (income, commodities, and assets)
3. According to Mary Robinson, former UN High Commissioner for Human Rights, a rights-based approach is a conceptual framework for the process of human development that is normatively based on international human rights standards and operationally directed at promoting and protecting human rights.
4. Cohen, Manion, et al. (2003).
5. Angola's original role with regards to the Portuguese Empire was as a supply point on the sea routes to Asia. To understand more about Angola's historical facts, read Duffy, J. (1959), Birmingham, D. (1965), Chabal, P. (2002).
6. The right to self-determination is defined as the free choice of one's own acts without external compulsion and especially as the freedom of the people of a given territory to determine their own political status or independence from their current state. See Chapter One of both the International Covenant on Civil and Political Rights (ICCPR) and the International Covenant on Economic Social and Cultural Rights (ICESCR)

7. United Nations, Resolution 1514 (XV) "Declaration on the Granting of Independence to Colonial Countries and Peoples," December 14, 1960, http://daccessdds.un.org/doc/RESOLUTION/GEN/NR0/153/48/IMG/NR015348.pdf?OpenElement.

8. Trotsky's exposure of the betrayal of the Chinese revolution in the 1920s by the Stalinist leaders contains one of the most important strategic lessons. In complete contrast to Trotsky's analysis, Stalin had claimed that the nationalist movement in China—the Kuomintang—would lead a democratic revolution against the feudal warlords and imperialist domination. This was also carried out amidst a huge campaign to denigrate Trotsky and his supporters.

9. The PCA was formed in 1953 and the PLUA in early 1956 Warnshuis (1923).

10. The MPLA has been in power since 1975 when Angola gained its independence from Portugal.

11. António de Oliveira Salazar was a dictator in Portugal who founded and led the Estado Novo ("New State"), the authoritarian, right-wing government that controlled Portugal's social, economic, cultural, and political life from 1932 to 1974.

12. Guinea Bissau's PAIGC was the first to proclaim independence, followed by FLELIMO in Mozambique.

13. Simultaneously, the FNLA and UNITA proclaimed a separate independence with headquarters in the southern city of Huambo. However, the two movements failed to set up a government until December 1975 and their independence failed to gain any formal recognition from the international community and other African countries. Hence, by January 1976, with the support of Cuban troops and Soviet arms, the MPLA had emerged as the sole dominant military power in Angola.

14. President Jose Eduardo dos Santos is the current President and Commander-in-Chief of the Armed Forces of Angola

15. Dr. Savimbi, the leader of UNITA, was strongly supported by the influential, conservative Heritage Foundation. The Foundation and other American conservatives provided Savimbi with ongoing political and military guidance in his

war against the MPLA government. Savimbi's U.S.-based supporters ultimately proved successful in convincing the Central Intelligence Agency (CIA) to channel covert weapons and recruit guerrillas for Savimbi's war against Angola's Marxist government, which greatly intensified and prolonged the conflict (Isaksen 2006).

16. For an in-depth understanding of the Bicesse Peace Agreement, see Hart and Lewis (1995); Higdon and Safeworld (1996); Krska (1997); Hare (1998); Halperin and Lomasney (1999).

17. Further information about when and how long a party was in power can be found at: African Political Resources (http://www.politicalresources.net/africa.htm) and Africa Election Database (http://africanelections.tripod.com/index.html).

18. The 1998 Global Witness report revealed the role of diamonds in funding the continuing civil war.

19. In September 2002, the Angolan government and UNITA re-established the Lusaka Protocol's Joint Commission to resolve outstanding political issues. On November 21, 2002, the Angolan government and UNITA declared the provisions of the Lusaka Protocol fully implemented and called for the lifting of sanctions on UNITA imposed by the United Nations Security Council (Griffiths 2004; Lopes 2004; Meijer 2004; Meijer and Birmingham 2004).

20. The 2003 OHCHR and the 2000 UNDP reports clearly explain the connections of human rights with poverty reduction and human development paradigms.

21. 2003 World Development Report, "Sustainable Development in a Dynamic Economy: Transforming Institutions, Growth, and Quality of Life."

22. Socialist Democracy, http://www.socialistdemocracy.org/index.html.

23. Looking at the volume of refugee flows for the last two decades, the first eighty-seven cases occurred in non-democratic societies (Sen 1999).

24. For detailed understanding of methods for data collection see Robson (2003); Sayer (2003); Smith (2003).

25. Por uma Angola Democratica (For a Democratic Angola), Open Society, Hotel Alvalde, Luanda, 2004.

26. Conference organized by UNDP and the Angolan Ministry of Justice over the theme of commission of justice and human rights reform in Angola, Luanda, May 2004.

27. Conference organized by the Open Society in Angola over the topic challenges to democracy in Angola, Luanda.

28. Conference organized by the Inter-church Committee for Peace in Angola (COEPA) and the Minister of Territorial Administration over the theme of reconciliation and peace building in Angola. Luanda, October 31 to November 4, 2005.

29 In Angola, there is one state-run news agency, the "Journal de Angola" and six private news agencies. The only daily newspaper is *Journal de Angola*, the private newspapers come out on a weekly basis, at weekends. Although the *Journal de Angola* makes mostly propaganda for government activities, the private newspapers are quietly critical and helped me to find another version of the information.

30. Content analysis is a social science method that consists of studying the content of communication. SeeWeber, R. P. (1990);Roberts, C. W. (1997); Krippendorff, K. (2004)

31. For a detailed explanation of the triangulation method read the works such as by O'Donoghue, T. and K. Punch (2003). Qualitative Educational Research in Action eBook.

32. "Gender Equality in Angola," http://www.wikigender.org/wiki/index.php?title=Gender_Equality_in_Angola#Family_Code.

33. Utilitarianism is the idea that the moral worth of an action is solely determined by its contribution to overall utility, that is, its contribution to happiness or pleasure as summed among all persons, meaning that the moral worth of an action is determined by its outcome—the ends justify the means. See Rosen 2003.

34. Libertarianism is a term used by a broad range of political philosophies that prioritise individual liberty and seek to minimise or even abolish the state. See Rothbard 1997.

35. Angola ratified the International Covenant on Political and Civil Rights on January 10, 1992. The articles of the ICCPR relevant to freedom of expression, assembly, and association are: Article 19 (1): Everyone shall have the right to hold opinions without interference; and 19 (2): Everyone shall have the right to freedom of expression; this right shall include the freedom to

seek, receive, and impart information and ideas of all kinds, regardless of frontiers, either orally, in writing or in print, in the form of art, or through any other media of his choice. Article 21: The right of peaceful assembly shall be recognized. No restrictions may be placed on the exercise of this right other than those imposed in conformity with the law and which are necessary in a democratic society in the interests of national security or public safety, public order, the protection of public health or morals or the protection of the rights and freedoms of others. Article 22 (1): Everyone shall have the right to freedom of association with others, including the right to form and join trade unions for the protection of his interests.

36. Angola ratified the African Charter on Human and People's Rights on March 2, 1990.

37. Fieldwork (2005). Anonymous interviews with members of oppositions parties in Luanda, Angola.

38. Arguably, OMA's most significant achievements occurred in the 1980s. Their efforts led to the introduction of the Family Code and formulation and implementation of a policy to provide free family planning to women. The main features of the Family Code are the recognition of consensual unions as marriage, the protection of children born out of wedlock, and the encouragement of a fair division of tasks and responsibilities within the family. OMA also provided technical assistance to women and encouraged debate and discussion on previously taboo subjects such as customary marriage and abortion.

39. One year before the 2002 cease-fire, Angola had 4.1 million displaced persons and 470,600 refugees (Loughna and Nicholson 2000). Thousands of displaced Angolans people and refugees have voluntarily returned to their homes since the ceasefire.

40. This situation was evident with the September 2008 legislative election where the MPLA won the majority of the seats in National Assembly.

41. Larger numbers of women living in extreme poverty have been displaced, lost their houses, husbands, and children in the war. These women are left with little hope for immediate improvement of their living conditions considering their low

level of education and the fact that little is done politically to address their special needs.

42. Fieldwork notes (2004). Informal conversation with Alberto a former combatants from FAPLA about human security in the post-conflict Luanda, Angola.

43. The HDI is an index combining normalised measures of life expectancy, literacy, educational attainment, and GDP per capita for countries worldwide.

44. http://www.unhchr.ch/html/menu6/2/fs22.htm. "The human rights of women and of the girl-child are an inalienable, integral, and indivisible part of universal human rights. The full and equal participation of women in political, civil, economic, social and cultural life, at the national, regional and international levels, and the eradication of all forms of discrimination on grounds of sex are priority objectives of the international community."

45. For better understanding of the concepts "market power" or "monopoly," read Maunder et al. (2000); Brickley, et al. (2003).

46. On the one side, UNITA kept civilian population captive, using them as gatekeepers, forced recruits, and human shields. On the other side, the Armed Forces of Angola (FAA) moved people to deprive UNITA of support (MSF 2002). In certain regions, it was very difficult for humanitarian organizations to reach these populations. As a result, the living conditions of people were difficult, which resulted in preventable deaths.

47. The au

48. Fieldwork observations.

49. United Nations, Resolution 217 A (III), "Universal Declaration of Human Rights," December 10, 1948, accessed August 02, 2007, http://www.un.org/Overview/rights.html.

50. In addition to these two sources, both the United Nations Declaration on Social Progress and Development (1969) and the United Nations Vancouver Declaration on Human Settlements (1976) recognize the rights of everyone to adequate housing.

51. Reports by human rights organizations, namely Amnesty International (AI), Human Rights Watch (HRW), and the Angolan organization SOS denounced forced eviction and demolition of houses in Boa-vista.

52. For an in-depth understanding of the impact of air pollution on health, the work by Professor Hester (2000) is worth to reading.
53. For example, it is against the law in United Kingdom and others Western countries to recruit expatriates for the position that could otherwise filled by local people.
54. This is evidence that international organizations in Angola do not fully comply with the international labor standards. These organizations are at grave violation of the paragraph 2(b)(v) of the ILO Discrimination (Employment and Occupation) Recommendation, 1958 (No. 111)—Article 23.2 of the "Universal Declaration of Human Rights" and Article 15 of the African Charter that stipulates the right for everyone, without any discrimination, to equal pay for equal work.
55. *Afro News*, "Luanda Most Expensive City in the World," October 10, 2008, http://www.afrol.com/articles/29519.
56. The mission of the Women's Commission for Refugee Women and Children is to improve the lives and defend the rights of refugee women and children, including the internally displaced, returnees, and asylum seekers (http://www.womenscommission. org/).
57. Informal conversation and e-mail exchange with Jose Silva about the situation of education in Angola, 2007.
58. GNI is the sum of value added by all resident producers plus any product taxes (less subsidies) not included in the valuation of output plus net receipts of primary income (compensation of employees and property income) from abroad. Data are in current international dollars.
59. The global financial crisis began in July 2007 when a loss of confidence by investors in the value of securitised mortgages in the United States resulted in a liquidity crisis that prompted a substantial injection of capital into financial markets by the United States Federal Reserve, Bank of England, and the European Central Bank. In September 2008, the crisis deepened, as stock markets worldwide crashed and entered a period of high volatility, and a considerable number of banks, mortgage lenders, and insurance companies failed in the following weeks.
60. "ISS Angola's Economy," http://www.iss.co.za/Af/profiles/ Angola/Econ.html.

61. Angola is the third largest producer of diamonds in Africa and has only explored 40 percent of the diamond-rich territory within the country. Despite increased corporate ownership of diamond fields, much production is currently in the hands of small-scale prospectors, often operating illegally. Only eight large-scale mines are operating out of a total of 145 concessions.

62. International diamond companies included Alrosa Company Ltd. (ALROSA) of Russia; BHP Billiton World Exploration Inc. and New Millenium Resources N.L. of Australia; Daumonty Financing Company B.V. of Israel (which was part of the Lev Leviev Group of Israel); De Beers Group, Petra Diamonds Ltd., and Trans Hex Ltd. of South Africa; Odebrecht Mining Services Inc. (Odebrecht) of Brazil; Pangea Diamondfields plc of the United Kingdom; and SouthernEra Diamonds Inc. of Canada.

63. "Business Monitor International's Angola Mining Report," http://www.businessmonitor.com/mining/angola.html.

64. "InterAction Member Activity Report on Angola, A Guide to Humanitarian and Development Efforts of InterAction Member Agencies in Angola," http://www.interaction.org/files.cgi/829_Angola_September_2002.pdf.

65. High inflation has many costs: Inflation erodes the value of money. Inflation can mean particular hardship for those whose incomes don't keep pace with the rising level of prices, especially people on fixed incomes such as senior citizens who are receiving pensions. http://www.bank-banque-canada.ca/en/backgrounders/bg-i2.html.

66. Broad money is considered to be the most inclusive means of measuring the state of the money supply in a given country or world market. It encompasses all sorts of financial information, and is considered to be the most comprehensive means of ascertaining the true financial condition of a nation or a market. An understanding of broad money can make a substantial impact on the decisions of investors to consider investments in the way of bonds and other securities that are relevant to that market.

67. "African Economic Outlook 2005-2006," www.oecd.org/dev/publications/africanoutlook.

68. IMF, "Angola: Selected Issues and Statistical Appendix," Country Report No. 05/125 (April 2005), 41. The debt in Angola is public or publicly guaranteed and is a liability of either the central government or Sonangol.
69. IMF, "Angola: 2006 Article IV Consultations, Preliminary Conclusions of the IMF Mission, No. 5. "
70. The Paris Club is an informal group of official creditors whose role is to find coordinated and sustainable solutions to the payment difficulties experienced by debtor nations. Paris Club creditors agree to rescheduling debts. Rescheduling is a means of providing a country with debt relief through a postponement and, in the case of concessional rescheduling, a reduction in debt service obligations. http://www.clubdeparis.org/sections/qui-sommes-nous.
71. The resource curse theory explains the paradox that countries with abundant natural resources tend to have less economic growth than countries without these natural resources. It has been articulated in this thesis that the basic objective of democracy is to produce governance capable of promoting and protecting the well-being of people. For detailed explanation of issues related to the resource curse theory, see Auty, R. M. (1993); Robinson, J. A., R. Torvik, et al. (2002); Boschini, A. D., J. Pettersson, et al. (2003); Kim, Y. (2003); Murshed, S. M. (2004); Rosser, A. (2006); Kolstad, I. (2007).
72. It is extremely difficult to definitively say that Dutch disease is the cause of the decreasing manufacturing sector, since there are many other factors at play in the economy. While it most often refers to natural resource discovery, it can also refer to "any development that results in a large inflow of foreign currency, including a sharp surge in natural resource prices, foreign assistance, and foreign direct investment." See Barritt, E. E. (1979).
73. Under EITI, state oil companies would also report what they receive from companies and pay governments, while governments are to report revenues received from the private sector and state-owned natural resource companies. This architecture is intended to create a web of double-entry checks.

74. World Bank, "Business Environment Snapshot for Angola," http://rru.worldbank.org/BESnapshots/Angola/default.aspx.

75. ANIP's mission is to help carry out government policies designed to support the growth of a diversified, stable economy that allows Angola to participate more fully in the global economy.

76. "Doing Business, 2007-2008's Ranking," http://www.doingbusiness.org/economyrankings/.

77. The Capanda Dam is a dam of the Kwanza River in Malanje Province, Angola. It is used by the Capanda hydroelectric power plant, and it is an important source of electricity for Angola.

78. World Bank, "Doing Business: Angola," http://www.doingbusiness.org/ExploreEconomies/?economyid=7.

79. Energy Information Administration, "Angola," http://www.eia.doe.gov/emeu/cabs/Angola/pdf.pdf.

80. GRN was set up in 2005 to manage large investment projects and ensure rapid infrastructure reconstruction prior to national elections. Headed by a military adviser to the president, General Helder Vieira Dias "Kopelipa," GRN was designed to provide work for demobilized military in order to bring new dynamism to the reconstruction effort. GRN is exclusively accountable to the Angolan presidency.

81. General Miala was dismissed from the army and sentenced on September 20, 2007 to four years in jail for insubordination.

82. Jose Pedro de Morais was appointed minister of Finance on December 9, 2002, by Angolan president, Jose Eduardo dos Santos. Edward George, analyst of *The Economist*, argued that the rapid economic growth of Angola was a result of the recommendation made by José Pedro de Morais, who advised the country to halt consultations with the International Monetary Fund (IMF) over the monitored program.

83. For example, the August 2007 IMF report praised the government's macroeconomic policies.

84. http://www.fao.org/faostat/foodsecurity/Countries/EN/Angola_e.pdf. The UN Food and Agriculture Organization estimates that 40 percent of Angolans are undernourished.

85. World Bank, "Angola at a Glance," (August 24, 2005), http://devdata.worldbank.org/AAG/ago aag.pdf; Population

Reference Bureau, "2005 World Population Data Sheet," http://www.prb.org/pdf05/05WorldDataSheet_Eng.pdf.

86. Good governance is, among other things, participatory, transparent, and accountable. It is also effective and equitable. And it promotes the rule of law. Good governance ensures that political, social, and economic priorities are based on broad consensus in society and that the voices of the poorest and the most vulnerable are heard in decision-making over the allocation of development resources.

87. Jornal de Angola, (terça-feira, April 14, 2009), Discurso do President da República na abertura da Conferência Nacional sobre Desenvolvimento Urbano e Habitacional.

88. UNPD, "Governance for Sustainable Human Development," http://meltingpot.fortunecity.com/lebanon/254/cheema.htm.

89. A "stable Angola" can be described as an Angola where there is an equilibrium between economic growth and human development.

90. Political trust can be direct toward the political system and its organizations as well as the individual political incumbents. The first category of political trust is refers to an issue-oriented perspective whereby citizens become trustful or distrustful of government "because they are satisfied or dissatisfied with policy alternative" (Miller 1974, 951). While organizational trust refers to the citizens' evaluation of the performance of the overall political system and regime, the individual trust involves a person-oriented perspective whereby citizens become trustful or distrustful of government "because of their approval or disapproval of certain political leaders" (Citrin 1974, 974-75). Both the organizational and individual political trust depends on credible policy making.

91. Observers from the 15-nation Southern African Development Community said the vote was "peaceful, free, transparent and credible" and reflected "the will of the people" (guardian.co.uk, http://www.guardian.co.uk/world/2008/sep/09/6).

92. These difficulties have certainly undermined Angolan hopes that the election would set a shining example of polls in Africa after defective elections in Kenya and Zimbabwe.

93. Business Anti-Corruption Portal, "Angola Country Profile," http://www.business-anti-corruption.com/normal.asp?pageid=386.

94. More than three quarters of African countries had organized respectively more than one time legislative elections; more than two-thirds of them had respectively held presidential elections three or four times (The International Institute for Democracy and Electoral Assistance, http://www.idea.int/about/.)

95. The National Assembly may review the Constitutional Law and approve the Constitution of the Republic of Angola on the decision of two-thirds of members present (Constitution of Angola, Article 158.1).

96. Methods for data collection and analysis were discussed in the Chapter I.

97. Unattributed interview (2004). Fieldwork interviews with a member of human rights organization in Luanda, Angola.

98. Unattributed interview (2004). Fieldwork interviews with journalist of Radio Ecclesia Luanda, Angola.

99. Participant in the informal conversation in Luanda.

100. Unattributed interview (2005). Fieldwork informal conversations with Alfoso, a security guard of "Guarda Seguro," Luanda, Angola.

101. Constitution of Angola, Article 66.

102. Unattributed interview (2004). Fieldwork interviews with a minister of the Angolan Government, Luanda, Angola.

103. Unattributed interview (2004). Fieldwork interviews with journalist of Radio Ecclesia Luanda, Angola.

104. For detailed explanation of widespread practice of corruption and clientelism, read the Human Right Watch, Global Witness, and IMF reports, as well as Walsh, D. (2002).

105. According to a 2004 Global Witness' report, nearly $1.7 billion disappeared from the government's budget between 1997 and 2001. While Angola's finances were certainly opaque during this time period, some Africa experts note the Global Witness report is controversial and the Angolan government did make efforts following its publication to account for the lost funds.

106. More information about the Angola Finance Ministry can be found at http://www.minfin.gv.ao/.

107. The 2006 World Bank report outlines some of these changes in detail (http://www-wds.worldbank.org/external/default/WDSContentServer/WDSP/IB/2006/10/24/000090341_20061024104820/Rendered/PDF/35362.pdf).

108. The Center for Preventive Action (CPA) was established by the Council on Foreign Relations in 1994 to help prevent, defuse, or resolve deadly conflicts around the world and to expand the body of knowledge on conflict prevention.

109. The United Nations Convention against Corruption was adopted by the United Nations General Assembly on October 31, 2003 (Resolution 58/4) to combat corruption. It includes measures on: prevention, criminalization, international cooperation, and asset recovery. The treaty entered into force on December 14, 2005, following the 30th ratification by Ecuador on September 15 at the 2005 World Summit. Further information can be found at: http://www.unodc.org/unodc/en/treaties/CAC/index.html.

110. The African Union Convention on Preventing and Combating Corruption (AU Convention) was adopted in Maputo on July 11, 2003. It represents regional consensus on what African states should do in the areas of prevention, criminalization, international cooperation, and asset recovery. Further information can be found at: http://www.africa-union.org/root/au/Documents/Treaties/treaties.htm.

111. An Extractive Industries Transparency Initiative (or EITI) sets a global standard for companies to publish what they pay and for governments to disclose what they receive. Further information can be found at: http://eitransparency.org/node.

112. An outline of the strategy, and the thinking behind it, can be found at http://www.mapess.gv.ao/temas/indicativo_governo1.htm.

113. "2007 Transparency International Corruption Perceptions Index," http://www.transparency.org/policy_research/surveys_indices/cpi/2010/results.

114. "Angola: Election, What Election," *Africa Confidential*, 45(24): 1-8.

115. Fieldwork notes (2005). Fieldwork informal conversations with Ricardo a former combattant and currently an employee in a security compagny (Guarda Seguro) Luanda, Angola.

116. Although the idea of redistributing land in Zimbabwe is not bad as such, the methods used by President Mugabe are rather questionable. Therefore, one could argue that land distribution in Zimbabwe was used strategically by the president to attract support of the minority influential people and starve the majority of ordinary citizens.

117. President Festus Mogae of Botswana gave up power to his vice president before the end of his second term.

118. The Freedom House Annual Survey employs the Political Rights checklist to help determine the degree to which people can participate in the political process of their country. Each country is then rated on a seven-category scale, 1 representing the most free and 7 the least free. These 7 categories are laid out below.

119. The Freedom House Annual Survey employs a civil liberties checklist to help monitor the progress and decline of human rights worldwide. Each country is rated on a seven-category scale, 1 representing the most free and 7 the least free. These 7 categories are laid out below.

120. Transparency International (TI) defines corruption as "the abuse of entrusted power for private gain." The TI seeks to provide reliable quantitative diagnostic tools regarding levels of transparency and corruption, both at global and local levels. Corruption Perceptions Index (CPI) ordering world's nation according to "the degree to which corruption is perceived to exist among public officials and politicians."

121. Comment by a member the Angolan government interview during the fieldwork in Angola.

122. The Botswana Democratic Party has been in power since independence of Botswana in 1965.

123. The ANC asked President Mbeki to step down days after a high court judge suggested that he may have interfered in a corruption case against his rival, ANC leader Jacob Zuma.

124. World Audit presents and updates the World Democracy ranking based on statistics and reports from highly respected agencies, each with their own developed specialties. Freedom House, Transparency International, Amnesty International, Human Rights Watch, and The International Commission of Jurists are

the names where political rights, civil liberties, press freedom, perceptions of corruption, human rights, and the rule of law are concerned. Further information about World Audit can be found at http://www.worldaudit.org/democracy.htm.

125. Selected authors on democratic education: McQuoid-Mason, D. J. (1994); Tamir, Y. (1995); Guarasci, R. and G. H. Cornwell (1997); Gutman, A. (1999); Roth, K. (2001); Skovsmose, O. and P. Valero (2001); Beach, D., T. Gordon et al. (2003); Blacker, D. J. (2007).

126. Resource rent is the difference between the price at which an output from a resource can be sold and its respective extraction and production costs, including normal return. In practice, resource rent depends on the availability of information, market conditions, technology and the system of property rights used to govern access to and management of resources. See T. E. and J. E. Richards (1987); Faber, M. and J. L. R. Proops (1991); Adner, R. and P. Zemsky (2002); Bjorvatn, K. (2007).

REFERENCES

A Capital. 2004. O Mundo escuro da Seguranca privada em Angola, A Fonte do Dinhero dos Generais, Um mercado exclusivo para Militares e Fimiliares.

Abdellatif, A. M. 2003. "Global Forum III on Fighting Corruption and Safeguarding Integrity. Good Governance and Its Relationship to Democracy and Economic Development." Seoul, South Korea. United Nations Development Programme. Programme on Governance in the Arab Region (POGAR).

Adamolekun, L. 1998. "Political Leadership in Sub-Saharan Africa: From Giants to Dwarfs." *International Political Science Review/ Revue internationale de science politique* 92: 95-106.

Adedeji, A. 1999. *Comprehending and Mastering African Conflicts: The Search for Sustainable Peace and Good Governance*. New York: Zed Books.

Adeniran, W. 2003. *Democracy and Military Dictatorship in Africa*. Lagos: Shalom Goldlinks Concept.

Adner, R., and P. Zemsky. 2002. *Strategy Dynamics through a Demand-Based Lens: The Evolution of Market Boundaries, Resource Rents, and Competitive Positions*. London: Centre for Economic Policy Research.

AFDB/OECD. 2007. "Angola: African Economic Outlook 2006-2006."

Accessed July 26, 2006. www.oecd.org/dev/publications/ africanoutlook.

Afigbo, A., and Ngũgĩ wa Thiong'o, 1977. *The Poverty of African Historiography*. Lagos: Afrografika.

Africa Confidential. 2008. "Angola: Stand and Deliver." *Africa Confidential* 49(19).

Agora. 2005. *Racismo no Bingo: Discoteca de mulatos e brancos Agora*. Luanda.

Aguilar, Renato. 2004. *Angola 2004: Getting off the Hook,* Stockholm: Sida.

AI (Amnesty International). 2003. "Angola: Mass Forced Evictions in Luanda—A Call for a Human-Rights Based Housing Policy." Amnesty International. Accessed August 12, 2007. http://web.amnesty.org/library/Index/ENGAFR120072003.

———. 2003. "Report 2004: Angola." Accessed July 27, 2007. http://web.amnesty.org/report2004/ago-summary-eng.

———. 2004. "Report on Angola." Amnesty International. Accessed September 1, 2007. http://web.amnesty.org/report2004/ago-summary-eng.

———. 2006. "Angola: Call on Government to End Forced Evictions and Excessive Use of Force Immediately." Amnesty International. AFR 12/04/2006.

———. 2006. "Angola: Human Rights Organization Banned." Amnesty International. August 4. . http://web.amnesty.org/library/Index/ENGAFR120062006?open&of=ENG-2F3.

———. 2008a. "Angola: Briefing for Election Monitors." Amnesty International. Accessed September 22, 2008. http://www.amnesty.org/en/library/info/AFR12/002/2008/en.

———. 2008b. "Angola: Intimidation." Amnesty International. Accessed September 22, 2008. http://www.amnesty.org/en/library/info/AFR12/007/2008/en.

———. 2008c. "Angola: Open Letter to Candidates to the National Assembly and Political Party Leaders: A Human Rights Agenda for Political Parties and Candidates in Parliamentary Elections." Amnesty International. Accessed September 22, 2008. http://www.amnesty.org/en/library/info/AFR12/003/2008/en.

———. 2008d. "Angola: Stop the Continued Harassment, Intimidation and Closure of Human Rights Organizations." Amnesty International. Accessed September 22, 2008. http://www.amnesty.org/en/library/info/AFR12/006/2008/en.

AlertNet, R. A. 2002. "Corruption Undermines Relief to Angola." Accessed October 17, 2007. http://www.alertnet.org/thefacts/reliefresources/544536.htm.

Alley, P., and A. Yearsley. 1999. "Angola: Diamonds Are a War's Best Friend." *AfricaFiles* 5(1): 10.

Almeida, H. 2008. "Angola Could Become an Agricultural Powerhouse." Reuters. Accessed September 12, 2008. http://africa.reuters.com/wire/news/usnLE242184.html.

Ammassari. 2005. *Migration and development: new strategic outlooks and practical ways forward: the cases of Angola and Zambia.* Geneva: International Organization for Migration

Bruce Baker. 2002. *Taking the Law into Their Own Hands: Lawless Law Enforcers in Africa.* Aldershot: Ashgate.

Amundsen, I., and C. Abreu. 2006a. *Angola: Civil Society as Promoters of Governance and Accountability.* Bergen, Norway: Chr. Michelsen Institute.

Amundsen, I., and C. Abreu. 2006b. *Civil Society in Angola: Inroads, Space, and Accountability.* Bergen, Norway: Chr. Michelsen Institute.

Amundsen, I., C. Abreu, and L. Hoygaard. 2005. *Accountability on the Move: The Parliament of Angola.* Bergen, Norway: Chr. Michelsen Institute.

Anand, S., and M. Ravallion 1993. "Human Development in Poor Countries: On the Role of Private Incomes and Public Services." *The Journal of Economic Perspectives* 7(1).

Anand, Z. 2003. *Sustainable Development in a Dynamic World: Transforming Institutions, Growth, and Quality Of Life.* New York: Oxford University Press.

De Andrade, V. P. 2000. "Democratization and Governance in Angola." Paper present at Time for Renewed International Commitment to Peace in Angola: Lessons Learnt and Ways Forward, IDRC and Higher Institute for International Relations (ISRI), Maputo, Mozambique, June.

Angola Press. 2008. "Angola: Chinese Official Guarantees Railways Works Conclusion." Accessed September 2008. http://allafrica.com/stories/200808180056.html.

Angolan Constitution. Article 79 of the Constitutional Law 1992.

Angolense. 2002. "As pervesas escolhas de um Presidente quase vitalicio, O infatigavel 'jogador-treinador.'"*Angolense.*

Angolense. 2004. "Dos Santos aguardado para teste de democracia." *Angolense.* May 22-29.

Angolense. 2004. "Um Assassinato de Contornos Obscuros." *Angolense.*

Angolense. 2004. "Caso milionarios, Graca Campos Absolvido." SeminarioAngolense.

ANIP. 2007. "The Construction and Infrastructure Sector." Business Opportunities. Accessed August 10, 2007. http://www.iie-angola-us.org/construction.htm.

Anstee, M. 2005. *Lessons from the 1992 Elections. The Challenges for Free and Fair Elections in Angola*. London: The Royal Institute of International Affairs.

Archer, R. 1995. *Economic Democracy: The Politics of Feasible Socialism*. Oxford: Clarendon Press.

Arezki, R., and F. van der Ploeg. 2007. *Can the Natural Resource Curse Be Turned into a Blessing?: The Role of Trade Policies and Institutions*. London: Centre for Economic Policy Research.

Asmal, K., D. Chidester, and W. James, eds. *Nelson Mandela in His Own Words: From Freedom to the Future*. By Nelson Mandela. London: Little, Brown and Company. 2003.

Assembleia Nacional. 2005. Lei Electoral. Imprensa nacional -E.P., Diario da Republica. June 2005.

Assensoh, A. B. 1998. *African Political Leadership: Jomo Kenyatta, Kwame Nkrumah, and Julius K. Nyerere*. Malabar, FL: Krieger Publishing.

Aturupane, H., P. Glewwe, and Paul Isenman. 1994. "Poverty, Human Development, and Growth: An Emerging Consensus?" *The American Economic Review* 84(2): 244-249.

Auty, R. M. 1993. *Sustaining Development in Mineral Economies: The Resource Curse Thesis*. London: Routledge.

Azikiwe, A. 2008. "Africa Liberation Day and the Legacy of Global Anti-Imperialist Movements." Pan-African News Wire. Accessed September 23, 2008. http://www.workers.org/2008/world/africa_liberation_day_0529/.

Babu, B. R. 2000. *Development Strategies for Africa and Asia in the New Global Structure*. Denver: Academic Books.

Baker, B. 1998. "The Class of 1990: How Have the Autocratic Leaders of Sub-Saharan Africa Fared under Democratisation." *Third World Quarterly* 19(1).

Baker B. 2002. *Taking the Law into Their Own Hands: Lawless Law Enforcers in Africa*. Aldershot: Ashgate.

Barnett, D. 1973. Interview with Spartacus Monimambu, MPLA Commander and Member of the Politico-Military Coordinating Committee (CCPM). Interviews in depth: MPLA-Angola. Richmond, B.C., Liberation Support Movement, Information Centre.

Barro, R. J., and D. B. Gordon. 1983. "A Positive Theory of Monetary Policy in a Natural Rate Model." *The Journal of Political Economy* 91(4): 589-610.

Bureau of Democracy, Human Rights, and Labor. 2007. *Angola: Country Reports on Human Rights Practices—2006*. Bureau of Democracy, Human Rights, and Labor.

Beetham, D. 2003. *Defining and Measuring Democracy*. London: Sage.

Bekoe, D. A. O. 2006. *East Africa and the Horn: Confronting Challenges to Good Governance*. Boulder, CO: Lynne Rienner Publishers.

Bender, G. J. 1972. "The Limits of Counterinsurgency: An African Case." *Comparative Politics* 4(3): 331-360

Bennett, N. R., ed. 1968. *Leadership in Eastern Africa. Six Political Biographies. Boston University African Research Studies*. Boston: Boston University Press.

Benzoni, L., P. C. Dufresne, and R. Goldstein. 2005. *Can Standard Preferences Explain the Prices of out of the Money S&P 500 Put Options*. Cambridge: National Bureau of Economic Research.

Birmingham, D. 1965. *The Portuguese Conquest of Angola. Institute of Race Relations*. London: Oxford University Press.

Birmingham, D. 1999. *Portugal and Africa*. Basingstoke: Macmillan.

———. 2004. *Portugal and Africa*. London: University Press.

———. 2006. *Empire in Africa: Angola and Its Neighbors*. Athens, Ohio: Ohio University Press.

Bjerke, J. O. 2004. *Private Sector Developement Study Angola*. Oslo: Norwegian Agency for Development Cooperation.

Black, R. 1992. *Angola*. Oxford: Clio Press.

Blanchard, O. 2000. *Macroeconomics*. Upper Saddle River, NJ: Pearson/Prentice Hall.

Blaydes, L., and M. Kayser 2007. "Counting Calories: Democracy and Distribution in the Developing World." *International Studies Quarterly* 55 (2011), 887–908.

Blondel, J. 1968. "Party Systems and Patterns of Government in Western Democracies." *Canadian Journal of Political Science* 1(2): 180–203.

BMI 2008. *The Angola Mining Report 2008*. London: Business Monitor International.

Bogaards, M. 2004. "Counting Parties and Identifying Dominant Party Systems in Africa." *European Journal of Political Research* 43(2): 173-197.

Bohn, H. 1988. Why do we have nominal government debt? *Journal of Monetary Economics* 21:127–40.

Bonavena, N. P. 2005. "Constitucionalmente, nada permite que Dos Santos continue depois de 2007." Seminario Angolense 14.

Boswell, T., and C. K. Chase-Dunn. 2000. *The Spiral of Capitalism and Socialism: Toward Global Democracy*. Boulder, CO: Lynne Rienner Publishers.

Bratton, M., and N. Van de Walle. 1998. *Democratic Experiments in Africa: Regime Transitions in Comparative Perspective*. Cambridge: Cambridge University Press.

Bridgland, F. 1986. *Jonas Savimbi: A Key to Africa*. New York: Paragon House.

Brittain, V. 1993. "When Democracy Is Not Enough: Denying Angola's Electoral Result." *Southern Africa Report Archive* 8(3-4).

Broadman, H. G., and G. Isik 2007. *Africa's Silk Road: China and India's New Economic Frontier*. Washington, DC: World Bank.

Brown. 2009. *The Rise and Fall of Communism*. Ecco Press, HarperCollins; and Bodley Head, Random House.

BTI. 2007. "Angola: Country Report." Accessed August 1, 2007. http://www.bertelsmann-transformation-index.de/70.0.html?L=0.

Burchett, W. 1978. *Southern Africa Stands Up: The Revolutions in Angola, Mozambique, Zimbabwe, Namibia and South Africa*. New York: Urizen Books.

Burda, M. C., and C. Wyplosz 2005. *Macroeconomics: A European Text*. Oxford: Oxford University Press.

Burnell, P. J. 2000. *Democracy Assistance: International Co-Operation for Democratization*. London: Routledge.

Campos, I., and A. Vines. 2008. "Angola and China: A Pragmatic Partnership." Paper Presented at a CSIS Conference, Prospects for

Improving U.S.-China-Africa Cooperation. December 5, 2007. Accessed September 13, 2008. http://www.csis.org/media/csis/pubs/080306_angolachina.pdf.

Carbone, G. 2005. *'Populism' Visits Africa: The Case of Yoweri Museveni and No-Party Democracy in Uganda*. London: Development Research Centre, Crisis States Programme.

CCPR (Covenant on Civil and Political Rights). 2005. Communication No 1128/2002: Angola, April 15. CCPR/C/83/D/1128/2002. (Jurisprudence). Views of the Human Rights Committee under the Optional Protocol to the International Covenant on Civil and Political Rights. Eighty-third session Communication No. 1128/2002 Human Rights Committee, Eighty-third session United Nations.

CESCR (Committee on Economic, Social and Cultural Rights). 2000. "The Right to the Highest Attainable Standard of Health." November 8. E/C. Geneva, United Nations, Economic and Social Council.

Chabal, P. 2002. *The History of Postcolonial Lusophone Africa*. London: C. Hurst & Co Publishers.

Chatham House 2005. *The Challenges for Free and Fair Elections in Angola*. London: The Royal Institute of International Affairs.

Chatta-Chipepa, L. 2003. *Angola, Human Development Threats, A Programme of Action*. Braamfontein: Open Society Initiative for Southern Africa.

China Economic Net. 2007. "Hangxiao Steel Structure defends handling of $4.4b Angolan contracts." Accessed September 15, 2008. http://en.ce.cn/Business/Enterprise/200703/27/t20070327_10833876.shtml.

Churchill, W. S. 1990. *Thoughts and Adventures*. London: Cooper.

CIDCM (Centre for International Development and Conflict Management). 2005. "Polity IV Country Reports 2005: Angola." University of Maryland, Center for International Development and Conflict Management.

Cilliers, J., and C. Dietrich. 2000. *Angola's War Economy. The Role of Oil and Diamonds*. Pretoria: South Africa Institute for Security Studies.

Clark, D. A. "The Capability Approach: Its Development, Critiques, and Recent Advances." Accessed July 23, 2008. http://www.gprg.org/.

Cohen, Manion, et al. 2003. *Research Methods in Education*, London: Routledge Falmer.

Collelo. T. 1989. Angola, a Country Study. 3d edition. Library of Congress, Federal Research Division

Collelo, T., Ed. 1991. *Angola: A Country Study.* Washington, D.C.: The Library of Congress.

Cornwell, R. 1999. "Angola the Political and Diplomatic Scene." *Africa Watch: Central Africa on the Boil* 8(1).

Dahl, R. A. 1985. *A Preface to Economic Democracy.* Berkeley: University of California Press.

Dahl, A.1991. *Democracy and its Critics.* Yale University Press.

———. 1989. *Democracy and Its Critics.* New Haven: Yale University Press.

———. 2006. *A Preface to Democratic Theory.* Chicago: University Press.

Davidson, B. 1973. *In the Eye of the Storm: Angola's People.* New York: Doubleday Anchor.

de-Vletter, F. 2002. *Promoting the Urban Micro-enterprise Sector in Angola.* Luanda: IOM/UNDP.

Dietrich, C. 2004. "The Use of Regional Diamond Trading Platforms to Access Conflict Zones." *African Security Review* 13(1).

Ducados, H. 2004. "Angolan Women in the Aftermath of Conflict." Accessed October 03, 2008. http://www.c-r.org/our-work/accord/angola/women-conflict.php.

Dugger, C. W. 2008. "Governing Party in Angola Wins Election in a Landslide, Official Results Show." *New York Times.* Accessed September 20, 2008. http://www.nytimes.com/2008/09/10/world/africa/10angola.html.

Edozie, Rita Kiki. *Reconstructing the Third World of Democratization in Africa.* Lanham, Md.: University Press of America. 2006.

Edwards, M. 1970. *The State in the Modern World: A Short Study of the Significance and Function of the State in a Contemporary World.* London: Chester House Publications.

Endreassen, B. E. 2008. "Brief Introduction to Human Rights-based Approach to Development." Norvegen Center for Human Rights. Accessed July 14, 2008. http://www.ihmisoikeusliitto.fi/julkaisut/hrbad/andreassen.pdf.

Energy Information Administration. 2008. "Angola Energy Data, Statistics and Analysis— \Oil, Gas, Electricity, Coal." Country Analysis Brief. Accessed September 15, 2008. http://www.eia. doe.gov/emeu/cabs/Angola/pdf.pdf.

European Union. 2008. EU Election Observation Mission, Angola 5 September 2008 1.Final Report on the Parliamentary Elections

FAO 2005. "Right to Food." Roma, Food, and Agriculture Organization of the United Nations (FAO).

Feijo, C. 2005. "Nao faz sentido debater os mandatos." Seminario Angolense 15.

Fitzpatrick, T. 2002. "The Two Paradoxes of Welfare Democracy." *International Journal of Social Welfare* 11(2): 159 - 169.

Fitzpatrick, T. 2003. *After the New Social Democracy: Social Welfare for the Twenty-First Century*. Manchester: Manchester University Press.

Folha 8. 2005. "MPLA ataca Dos Santos." Luanda: 8-9.

Folha 8. 2005. "MPLA pode desintegrar-se, Os diamentes e o petróleo não foram a causa da guerre." Luanda: 2-3.

Francisco, T. 2004. O Mundo Escuro da Seguranca Privada em Angola: Um Mercado Exclusivo para Militares e Familiares. A Fonte do Dinheiro dos Generais. *A Capital* 106: 2.

Freedom House. 2006. "Country Report." Accessed January 15, 2007. http://www.freedomhouse.org/template.cfm?page=22&year=2006.

Freeman, M. 2002. *Human Rights: An Interdisciplinary Approach*. Oxford: Polity.

Friedman. 2005. *The World is Flat: A Brief History of the Twenty-first Century*. Farrar, Straus and Giroux; 1st edition.

Galli, R. E. 1987. "The Food Crisis and the Socialist State in Lusophone Africa." *African Studies Review* 30(1): 19-44.

Galtung, J. 1996. *Peace by Peaceful Means: Peace and Conflict, Development and Civilization*. London: Sage.

Gasha, J. G., and G. Pastor 2004. "Angola's Fragile Stabilization." IMF Working Paper., African Department JEL. Classification Numbers E52, E58, E65.

Gasper, D. 2007. "What is the Capacity Approach? Its Core, Rationale, Partners, and Dangers." *The Journal of Socio-Economics* 36: 335-359.

George, E. 2005. *The Cuban Intervention in Angola, 1965-1991: From Che Guevara to Cuito Cuanavale*. London: Routledge.

Gilbert, H. 2001. *Postcolonial Plays An Anthology*. London: Routledge.

Giliomee, H. 1996. *Liberal and Populist Democracy in South Africa: Challenges, New Threats to Liberalism*. Johannesburg: South African Institute of Race Relations.

Giliomee, and Simkins. 1999. *The Awkward Embrace; One Party-Domination and Democracy*. Tafelberg: Cape Town

Gjerstad, O. 1976. *The People in Power: An Account from Angola's Second War of National Liberation*. Oakland, CA: LSM Information Center.

Gleijeses, P. 2003. "Cuba and the Independence of Namibia." *Cold War History* 7(2): 285-303.

Global Witness. 2004. Time for Transparency. Accessed April 04, 2012, www.globalwitness.org.

Griffin, K., and J. B. Knight 1990. *Human Development and the International Development Strategy for the 1990s*. Basingstoke: Macmillan.

Gutmann. 1987. *Democratic Education*, Princeton. N.J.: Princeton University Press.

Haberler, G. 1981. *Schumpeter's Capitalism, Socialism, and Democracy after Forty Years*. Kyoto, Japan: Keibunsha.

Halebsky, S., J. M. Kirk, C. Bengelsdorf, R. L. Harris, J. Stubbs, and A. Zimbalist. 1992. *Cuba in Transition: Crisis and Transformation*. Oxford: Westview Press.

Hall, R. E., and J. B. Taylor 1991. *Macroeconomics: Theory, Performance and Policy*. New York: Norton.

Halperin, M. H., J. T. Siegle, and M. Weinstein. 2005. *The Democracy Advantage: How Democracies Promote Prosperity and Peace*. London: Routledge.

Hanhimeaki. 2004. *The Flawed Architect: Henry Kissinger and American Foreign Policy*. Oxford: Oxford University Press.

Hanson, S. 2008. "Angola's Political and Economic Development." Backgrounder. July 21. Accessed September 12, 2008. http://www.cfr.org/publication/16820/.

Haq, M. U. 1999. *Reflections on Human Development*. Oxford: Oxford University Press.

Harrigan, J. 2000. *From Dictatorship to Democracy: Economic Policy in Malawi 1964-2000.* Aldershot: Ashgate.

Hattersley, R. 1987. *Choose Freedom: The Future for Democratic Socialism.* London: Joseph.

Heidhues, P. 2004. Essays on microeconomic theory. *Habilitationsschrift.* Humboldt-Universität zu Berlin.

Herbertsson, T. T., and M. Skuladottir. 2000. *Three Symptoms and a Cure: A Contribution to the Economics of the Dutch Disease.* Centre for Economic Policy Research.

Hodges, T. 2001. *Angola from Afro-Stalinism to Petro-Diamond Capitalism.* Bloomington, Indiana; Indiana University Press.

Hodges, T. 2004. *Angola: Anatomy of an Oil State.* Bloomington, Indiana; Indiana University Press.

HRW (Human Rights Watch). 2003. "Angola: Resettlement Process Highly Flawed." Accessed July 26, 2007. http://www.hrw.org/reports/2003/angola0803/3.htm#_Toc47430855.

———. 2004. *Unfinished Democracy: Media and Political Freedoms in Angola.* New York: Human Rights Watch.

———. 2004. "Violation of the Right to Freedom of Expression, Arbitrary Imprisonment, Violence, and Threats against Journalists." Backgrounders. Accessed August 07, 2007. http://hrw.org/backgrounder/africa/angola/2004/5.htm#_ftnref66.

———. 2005. *Coming Home: Return and Reintegration in Angola.* Vol. 17(2). New York: Human Rights Watch.

———. 2006. "Cuba: Human Rights Concerns for the 61st Session of the U.N. Commission on Human Rights." Accessed December 19, 2007. http://hrw.org/english/docs/2005/03/10/cuba10306.htm.

———. 2006. *Rights to Freedom of Expression and Information under Angola's New Press Law.* Vol. 18(11). New York: Human Rights Watch.

———. 2007. "They Pushed Down the Houses: Forced Evictions and Insecurity of Tenure for Luanda's Urban Poor." Vol. 19(7).

———. 2008. "Angola: Doubts over Free and Fair Elections—Intimidation of Opposition, Media Before First Poll Since 1992." Human Rights News. Accessed September 21, 2008. http://www.hrw.org/english/docs/2008/08/13/angola19584.htm.

Hughes, A. 1992. *Marxism's Retreat from Africa.* London: Frank Cass.

Huse, M. D., and S. L. Muyakwa. 2008. "China in Africa: Lending, Policy Space and Governance." Norwegian Campaign for Debt Cancellation. Accessed September 18, 2008. http://www. slettgjelda.no.

Hvid, H., and P. Hasle 2003. *Human Development and Working Life: Work for Welfare.* Aldershot: Ashgate.

IDRC. 2005. "Projects in Angola. Human Security and the International Diamond Trade in Africa." Accessed September 06, 2008. http://www.crdi.ca/en/ev-66810-201_102008-1-IDRC_ADM_INFO. html.

IEA (International Energy Agency). 2006. "Angola: Towards an Energy Strategy." Accessed August 02, 2007. http://www.iea. org/w/bookshop/add.aspx?id=245.

IMF (International Monetary Fund). 2007. "Angola and the IMF." Accessed September 16, 2008. http://www.imf.org/external/country/ago/index.htm.

―――. 2003. "IMF Concludes 2003 Article IV Consultation with Angola Public Information Notice." (PIN) No. 03/114. International Monetary Fund.

Inglehart, R., and C. Welzel 2005. Modernization, Cultural Change, and Democracy: The Human Development Sequence. Cambridge: Cambridge University Press.

Integrated Framework. 2005

International Crisis, G. 2003. "Angola: Exorcising Savimbi's Ghost." Current History Index 101: 651-659.

IRI (International Republican Institute). 2006. "Republic of Angola National Opinion Poll." Accessed Sptember 10, 2008. http://www.iri.org/africa/angola/pdfs/2006-12-06-Angolan-Poll.pdf.

IRIN (Integrated Regional Information Networks). 2001. "Angola: Dos Santos to Bow Out." Accessed 15 September 2006. http://allafrica.com/angola/bydate/?n=8.

―――. 2001. "Dos Santos to Bow Out." August 24.

―――. 2003. "Angola: Dos Santos at the Helm." Accessed 12 September 2006. http://www.irinnews.org/advsearch.asp.

―――. 2003b. ANGOLA: Education drive receives government boost. Accessed April 04, 2012, http://www.irinnews.org/printreport.aspx?reportid=46928

————. 2004. "Angola: Post-war elections to Cost US $430 million." Accessed July 29, 2006. http://www.moneyandpolitics.net/news/pdf/Angola_6_30_OchaIRIN.pdf.

————. 2006a. "Angola: Easy access to Guns Concern as Election Nears." Accessed July 31, 2007. http://www.globalsecurity.org/military/library/news/2006/03/mil-060314-irin01.htm.

————. 2006b. "Angola: Oil rich but Dirt Poor." Maxist Thought Online. Accessed July 10, 2006. http://www.politicalaffairs.net/article/view/2548/1/144.

————. 2006c. "Angola: Uncertainty Increases over Election Date." Accessed September 15, 2006. http://www.irinnews.org/report.asp?ReportID=51752&SelectRegion=Southern_Africa&SelectCountry=ANGOLA.

————. 2007a. "Angola: A Year of Cholera Teaches Prevention is Better Than Treatment." Accessed August 10, 2007. http://www.irinnews.org/Report.aspx?ReportId=70019.

————. 2007b. "Angola: Govt on Greater Participation of Non-Oil Sector in GDP." Accessed August 1, 2007. http://allafrica.com/stories/200707270097.html.

————. 2007c. "Angola: Oil-backed Loan Will Finance Recovery Projects." Accessed July 31, 2007. http://www.irinnews.org/report.aspx?reportid=53112.

————. 2007d. "Angola: Political Climate Heats Up in Countdown to Elections." Accessed July 31, 2007. http://www.irinnews.org/report.aspx?ReportId=70595.

————. 2007e. "Angola: Uncertainty Increases over Election Date." Accessed August 1, 2007. http://www.irinnews.org/report.aspx?reportid=58168.

————. 2008a. "Angola: Election Free and Fair, Sort Of." Accessed September 29, 2008. http://www.irinnews.org/report.aspx?ReportId=80253.

————. 2008b. "Angola: Interview with Douglas Steinberg, CARE Country Director." Accessed September 29, 2008. http://www.irinnews.org/report.aspx?reportid=43248.

Jahan, S. 2002. *Human Development and Millennium Development Goals (MDGs): Analytical Linkages and Policy Issues.* New York.

Jaime, A. 2007. "Interview with the National Radio of Angola (RNA) Angola Press Agency." Luanda, Angola.

Johnson and Brock. 2009. "Angolan Oil Output to Surge over Next 5 years. Reuters.com." Accessed April 04, 2012, http://www.reuters.com/article/2009/11/09/us-oil-angola-surge-idUSTRE5A82TI20091109

Knight, M., and A. Ozerdem 2004. "Guns, Camps and Cash: Disarmament, Demobilization and Reinsertion of Former Combatants in Transitions from War to Peace." *Journal of Peace Research* 41(499).

Krška, V. 1997. "Peacekeeping in Angola (UNAVEM I and II)." *International Peacekeeping* 4(1).

Kuklys, W. 2005. *Amartya Sen's Capability Approach: Theoretical Insights and Empirical Applications*. Berlin: New York: Springer.

Kunnie, J. 2000. *Is Apartheid Really Dead?: Pan Africanist Working Class Cultural Critical Perspectives*. Boulder, CO: Westview Press.

Langford, M. 2000. "The United Nations Concept of Water as a Human Right: A New Paradigm for Old Problems?" *Water Resources Development* 21(2): 273-282.

Layard, P. R. G., S. J. Nickell, and R. Jackman. 2005. *Unemployment: Macroeconomic Performance and The Labour Market*. Oxford: Oxford University Press.

Leftwich, A. 1993. "Democratisation in the Third World." *Third World Quarterly* 14(3).

Lei no 2/05. 2005. Dos Partidos Politicos. - Revoga as Leis no 15/91 de Março, no 4/92 de 27 de Março e no 2/97 de 7 de Março, National Assembly.

Lei no 14/91. 1991. Sumula da legigislacao Approvada Pela Assembleia do Povo e Assembleia Nacional de Angola. I. S. Assembleia do Povo (Dr. no 20, de 11 de Maio) Das Associacoes, National Assembly.

Lindberg, S. I. 2006. *Democracy and Elections in Africa*. Baltimore: Johns Hopkins University Press.

Lipset, S. M., and S. Rokkan. 1967. *Party Systems and Voter Alignments: Cross-National Perspectives*. London: Collier Macmillan.

Lodge, T., D. Kadima, and D. Pottie, eds. 2002. *Angola: Post-Independence Compendium of Elections in Southern Africa.* Johannesburg: EISA.

López-Pinto, R., and J. Fischer. 2006. "How Much Do Elections Cost?" http://aceproject.org/ace-en/focus/core/crb/crb03/?searchterm=cost%20of%20elections.

Loughna, S., and F. Nicholson. 2000. *The State of the World's Refugees, Fifty Years of Humanitarian Action.* Oxford: University Press.

Mackenzie, L. 1989. *Facing the Challenges of the 1990s: Organising for Democracy in the Western Cape.* Bellville, South Africa: University of the Western Cape.

MacQueen, N. 1997. *The Decolonisation of Portuguese Africa: Metrolitan Revolution and Dissolution of the Empire.* London: Longman.

Magubane, K. 2008. "Economic Boomtime in Angola." Accessed September 02, 2008. http://www.mediaclubsouthafrica.com/index.php?option=com_content&view=article&id=698:angolas-economy-hits-20-growth&catid=47:africa_news&Itemid=57.

Mai, V. A., and F. G. Wisner. 2007. *Toward an Angola Strategy: Prioritizing U.S.-Angola Relations.* New York: The Center for Preventive Action.

Makidi-Ku-Ntima 1983. "Class Struggle and the Making of the Revolution in Angola." *Contemporary Marxism 6.* Institute for the Study of Labour and Economic Crisis.

Makumbe, J. M. 1999. *Democracy and Development in Zimbabwe: Constraints of Decentralisation.* Oxford: African Books Collective.

Malaquias, A. 2000. "Angola's Foreign Policy since Independence: The Search for Domestic Security." *African Security Review* 9(3).

Malaquias, A. 2007. *Rebels and Robbers: Violence in Post-Colonial Angola.* Uppsala, Sweden: Nordiska Afrikainstitutet.

Manning, C. 2005. "Assessing African Party Systems after the Third Wave." *Party Politics* 11(6): 707-27.

Marcum, J. 1969. *The Angolan Revolution: The Anatomy of an Explosion (1950-1962).* Cambridge: Cambridge Press.

Marcum, J. A. 1978. *The Angolan Revolution.* London: M.I.T. Press.

Markovic, M. 1982. *Democratic Socialism: Theory and Practice.* New York: St. Martins Press.

Marques, J. P. 2006. *The Sounds of Silence: Nineteenth-Century Portugal and the Abolition of the Slave Trade.* Oxford: Berghahn.

Marques, R. 2006. *The Power of Oil and the State of Democracy in Angola.* Harvard: Harvard Law School.

Matlosa, K. 2004. "Caught between Transition and Democratic Consolidation: Dilemmas of Political Change in Southern Africa." In *Southern Africa Post-Apartheid? The Search for Democratic Governance.* Edited by C. Landsberg and S. Mackay. Cape Town: IDASA.

McMilan. 2005. *The Main Institution in the Country Is Corruption: creating Transparency in Angola.* Stanford, Stanford University.

Meditz, S. W., and T. Merrill. 1994. *Zaire: A Country Study.* Washington, D.C.: Government Printing Office.

Meijer, G. 2004. *From Military Peace to Social Justice? The Angolan Peace Process.* London: Conciliation Resources.

Meijer, G., and D. Birmingham. 2004. "Angola from Past to Present." Conciliation Resources.

Meredith, M. 2005. *The Fate of Africa: A History of Fifty Years of Independence.* New York: Public Affairs.

Messiant, C. 2001. "The Eduardo dos Santos Foundation: How Angola's Regime is Taking Over Civil Society." *African Affairs* 100: 287-309.

Messiant, C. 2004. "Why did Bicesse and Lusaka Fail? A Critical Analysis." In *Military Peace to Social Justice? The Angolan Peace Process.* Edited by G. Meijer. London: Accor. 15.

Messiant, C. 2006. *L'Angola Post-colonial. Sociologie politique d'une oléocratie.* Paris: Karthala.

Minter, W. 1994. *Apartheid's Contras: An Inquiry into the Roots of War in Angola and Mozambique.* London: Zed Books.

Minter, W., and African-European Institute. 1995. *Account from Angola: UNITA as Described by Ex-participants and Foreign Visitors.* Amsterdam: AWEPAA.

Minter, W. 2002. Angola After Savimbi. *The Nation magazine.* Access April 04, 2012, http://www.thenation.com/issue/april-29-2002.

Mozaffar, Shaheen, et al. 2005. "The Puzzle of African Party Systems." *Party Politics* 11: 399-421.

MPLA (Popular Movement for the Liberation of Angola). "Estatus do MPLA." Accessed October 17, 2007. http://www.mpla-angola. org/estatutos_mpla.pdf.

———. 1972. *Revolution in Angola*. London: Merlin Press.

———. 1992. *O Future Certo. Manifesto Eleitora*. Luanda: Popular Movement for the Liberation of Angola.

———. 1995. "Tese o MPLA e os Desafios do Seculo XXI. IV Congresso Ordinario do MPLA." Accessed October 17, 2007. http://www.mpla-angola.org/congresos_realizados.php.

MPLA 1996. MPLA 40 ANOS Por Angola. Luanda, MPLA.

MSF. 2002. "Angola: As Peace Is Discussed, The Horrors of War Are Revealed, A Statement for the Record For the Committee on International Relations Subcommittee on Africa." Accessed August 8, 2007. http://www.doctorswithoutborders.org/ publications/speeches/2002/angola.htm.

Mueller, A. P. 2001. "Financial Cycles, Business Activity, and the Stock Market." *Quarterly Journal of Austrian Economics* 4(1).

Ndulo, M. 2006. *Democratic Reform in Africa: Its Impact on Governance and Poverty Alleviation*. Oxford: James Currey.

Neto, G. 2007. Foi-se a "Oposiçao Verdadeiramente Radical." *Angolense*. Luanda.

Neuberger, B. 1974. "Has the Single-Party State Failed in Africa?" *African Studies Review* 17(1): 173 -178.

Newman, E., and R. Rich. 2004. *The UN Role in Promoting Democracy: Between Ideals and Reality*. New York: United Nations University Press.

Newson, L. A., and S. Minchin 2007. "From Capture to Sale: The Portuguese Slave Trade to Spanish South America in the Early Seventeenth Century." *Atlantic World* 12.

N'Ganga, J. P. 2005. "A Demissao de Samakuva: As Responsabilidades da UNITA." *Folha 8*. Luanda, WT/Mundovideo, Lda 2-3.

Nkondo, M. 2005. "Kuangana corrige erro de Savimbi com denuncia antecipada, Registo de nascimento é feito pelo SINFO." *Folha 8*. Luanda.

Nyamu-Musembi, and Cornwall. 2004. 'What is the Rights-based Approach all about? Perspectives from International Development

Agencies', IDS Working Paper no. 234, Institute for Development Studies: Brighton.

OCHA. 2004. "Lessons Learned Review: OCHA-Angola 2000–2002." Accessed August 16, 2008. http://www.reliefweb.int/rw/rwb.nsf/AllDocsByUNID/968457e53f45a39a49256ed800053983.

O'Donnell, G. 1994. "Delegative Democracy." *Journal of Democracy*. (5)1: 55-69

OECD/IEA 2006. *Angola—Towards an Energy Strategy*. Viena: the International Energy Agency.

OHCHR (Office of the United Nations High Commissioner for Human Rights). 2007a. "International Convention on the Elimination of All Forms of Racial Discrimination." Accessed August 3, 2007. http://www.ohchr.org/english/law/cerd.htm.

———. 2007b. "International Covenant on Civil and Political Rights." New York: December 16, 1966 " Accessed July 25, 2007. http://www.ohchr.org/english/countries/ratification/4.htm.

———. 2007c. "Right to Adequate Housing." Accessed August 8, 2007. http://www.unhchr.ch/housing/fs21.htm#intro.

Okuma, T. 1962. *Angola in Ferment. The Background and Prospects of Angolan Nationalism*. Boston: Beacon Press.

Oliveira. 2007. Business success, Angola-style: postcolonial politics and the rise and rise of Sonangol. *The Journal of Modern African Studies*, 45:595-619.

Olson, M. 1993. "Dictatorship, Democracy, and Development." *American Political Science Review* 87(3): 567-576.

Osakwe. 2007. "Foreign Aid, Resources and Export Diversification in Africa: A New Test of Existing Theories." *MPRA Paper 2228*. University Library of Munich: Germany.

Ottaway 1997. *Democracy in Africa: The Hard Road Ahead. Boulder, Colo*. London: L. Rienner.

Pacheco, C. 1997. *MPLA: Um Nascimento Pole*. Lisboa: Vega.

Paguntke. 2002. "Parties without Firm Social Roots? Party Organizational Linkage." *Staffordshire, School of Politics, International Relations and the Environment (SPIRE)*, Keele University.

Painter, D. S. 1999." *The Cold War: An International History*. London: Routledge.

Panebianco, A. 1988. *Political Parties: Organization and Power*. Cambridge: Cambridge University Press.

Panitch, L. 1976. *Social Democracy and Industrial Militancy: the Labour Party, the Trade Unions and Income Policy 1945-1974*. Cambridge: Cambridge University Press.

Pei, M. 2001. *Future shock: The WTO and Political Change in China*. Washington, DC: Carnegie Endowment for International Peace

Pempel, T. J. 1990. "Uncommon Democracies: The One-Party Dominant Regimes." Conference Paper. Ithaca: Cornell University Press.

Pinto, I. 2005. "O PR so depende da propria vontade." Seminario Angolense 12.

Poelhekke, S., and F. van der Ploeg 2007. *Volatility, Financial Development and the Natural Resource Curse*. London: Centre for Economic Policy Research.

Population and Development Review. 1993. "Vienna Declaration on Human Rights." *Population and Development Review* 19(4): 877.

Quinault.1979. Lord Randolph Churchill and Tory Democracy, 1880–1885. *The Historical Journal*, 22:141-165

Rajkumar and Swaroop. 2002. *Public Spending and Outcomes: Does Governance Matter?* World BankWorking Paper No.: 2840.

Ramirez, A., and G. Ranis. 1997. "Economic Growth and Human Development." Economic Growth Center, Yale University.

Ranbanda, H. 1979. *Democratic Socialism*. Matale: Lankanatha Publishers.

Ranis et al. 1997. *Growth and Development from an Evolutionary Perspective*. Basil Blackwell.

Ranis et al. 2000. "Economic Growth and Human Development." *World Development*, February 2000, Vol. 28(2): 197-219.

Ranis, G. 2004. "Human Development and Economic Growth." Economic Growth Center, Yale University.

Ranis and Stewart. 2006. "Human Development: Beyond the Human Development Index." *Journal of Human Development*, 7 (3): 323-58.

Redvers, L. 2008. "Development-Angola: Building Sustainable Water Systems." Accessed October 04, 2008. http://www.ipsnews.net/africa/nota.asp?idnews=44087.

Reingold, J. 2004. "From Angola to Kazakhstan: How to Cure Corruption in Oil Rich States." Accessed September, 2008. http://www.upsidedownworld.org/ReingoldOil.htm.

ReliefWeb. 2004. "Angola Peace Monitor Issue No. 5, Vol. X." http://www.reliefweb.int/rw/rwb.nsf/db900sid/OCHA-64DCRB?OpenDocument.

Robson. 2003. *Real World Research*. Oxford: Blackwell Publishing.

Robert Ross 1982. "Review of A.H.M. Kirk-Greene *Africa in the Colonial Period III, The Transfer of Power: The Colonial Administrator in the Age of Decolonisation,*" *Itinerario*. 6, 156-157.

Rothchild, D., and C. Hartzell 1991. "Great- and Medium-Power Mediations: Angola." *Annals of the American Academy of Political and Social Science*. 518: 39-57.

Sachikonye, L. M. 2002. "Whither Zimbabwe? Crisis & Democratisation." *Review of African Political Economy* 29(91): 13-20.

Sala-i-Martin, X., and A. Subramanian 2003. *Addressing the Natural Resource Curse: An Illustration from Nigeria*. Cambridge, Mass., National Bureau of Economic Research.

Sano, H. O., and G. Alfredsson 2002. *Human Rights and Good Governance: Building Bridges*. London: Martinus Nijhoff.

Santana, A. 2005. "Racismo na Industria Petrolifera." *Folha 8*. Luanda: 10.

Santana, A. 2006. *Political Parties and Political Evolution in Angola*. Johannesburg: EISA.

Santos, O. d. 1992. *Eleiçoes Angolanas 1992: Uma Liçao para o Futuro*. Luanda: USAID.

Sartori, G. 1976. *Parties and Party Systems: A Framework for Analysis*. Cambridge: Cambridge University Press.

Sayer. 2003. *Method in Social Science: a realist approach.* London and New York. Routledge, Taylor and Francis Group.

Schedler, A., L. Diamond, and M. F. Plattner. 1999. *The Self-Restraining State: Power and Accountability in New Democracies*. Boulder, CO: Lynne Rienner Publishers.

Scully. 1998. "The Institutional Framework and Economic Development." *Journal of Political Economy*. 96(3): 652-662.

Sen, A. 1999. *Development as Freedom*. Oxford: Oxford University Press.

———. 2001a. "Democracy as a Universal Value." In *The Global Divergence of Democracies*. Edited by Larry Diamond and Marc F. Plattner. Washington D.C.: Johns Hopkins University Press.

———. 2001b. *Development as Freedom*. Oxford: Oxford University Press.

Shaxson, N. 2007. "Oil, Corruption, and the Resource Curse." *International Affairs* 83(6): 1123-1140.

Shaxson. 2008. "Angola's Homegrown Answers to the 'Resource Curse'." *Governance of Oil in Africa: Unfinished Business*. pp 52 – 102.

Shaxson, N., J. Neves, and F. Pacheco. 2008.

Simao, P. 2005. "Analysis-Angola Oil Boom Raises Political Fears." Accessed October 22, 2007. http://www.reuters.com/article/latestCrisis/idUSL30373618.

Smith. 2005. *Freedom's Distant Shores: American Protestants and Post-Colonial Alliances with Africa*. Waco, Texas: Baylor University Press.

Smith, B. C. 2007. *Good Governance and Development*. Basingstoke, Palgrave: Macmillan.

Smith, M. J. 2003. *Social Science in Question*. London: Thousand Oaks.

Somerville, K. 1986. *Angola: Politics, Economics and Society*. London: Pinter.

Southall, R. 2003. "Democracy in Southern Africa: Moving Beyond a Difficult Legacy." *Review of African Political Economy* 96: 255-272.

Southall, R., and H. Melber 2006. *Legacies of Power: Leadership Change and Former Presidents in African Politics*. Cape Town: HSRC Press.

Spence, M. 1978. *National Liberation and State Power: An Anarchist Critique of the MPLA in Angola*. Newcastle-upon-Tyne: Black Jake Collective.

Spence, M. 2007. "National Liberation and State Power: An Anarchist Critique of the MPLA in Angola." Black Jake Collective.

Spinola, A. D. 1974. *On Empowering the Governors of Angola and Mozambique*. Lisbon: Ministry of Mass Communication.

Summers, D., ed. 1995. Longman Dictionary of Contemporary English. T. Edition. London: Longman Group Ltd.

SWAPO. 1978. *Massacre at Kassinga: Climax of Pretoria's All-Out Campaign against the Namibian Resistance*. Windhoeck: South West Africa People's Organization.

Swisspeace. 2005. "FAST Update Angola: Semi-annual Risk Assessment Dec 2004 to May 2005." Accessed July 27, 2007. http://www.reliefweb.int/rw/rwb.nsf/db900SID/EVIU-6E7BLU?OpenDocument.

Tahri, J. E. 2007. *Cuba! Africa! Revolution!* Documentary. BBC Four.

Takirambudde, P. 2007. "Three Years after the End of Angola's Brutal Civil War, the Angolan Government Is Failing to Care for the Country's Huge Population of Returning Displaced Persons." Accessed August 13, 2007. http://hrw.org/english/docs/2005/03/17/angola10322.htm.

Tito, L. B. 2005. "Este é o terceiro e ultimo mandato de Jes." Seminario Angolense 13.

Toit, B. M. d. 1977. "Lunda under Belgian Rule: The Politics of Ethnicity." *American Anthropologist* 79(1): 154-155

Tomasevski, K. 2006. "The State of the Right to Education Worldwide." Accessed August 19, 2007. www.right-to-education.org.

Tonet, W. 2005. "Meu caro camarada President 30 anos de frustracao." *Folho 8*. Lunda: 2-3.

UNFPA (United Nations Population Fund). 2007. "Indicators/Policy Development: Angola." ———. "Worldwide: Population, Health & Socio-Economic Indicators/Policy Developments." Accessed August 02, 2007. http://www.unfpa.org/profile/compare.cfm.

UNHCR. 2002. "United Nations Haut Commessariat for Refugees." Statistical Yearbook 2001.

UNICEF (United Nations Children's Fund). 2006. "Cholera Outbreak Poses Additional Threat to Child Survival in Angola." Accessed August 5, 2007. http://www.unicef.org/infobycountry/media_33913.html.

———. 2006. "In Angola, Fresh Water Saves Many Threatened by Cholera Outbreak." Newsline. Accessed August 8, 2007. http://www.unicef.org/infobycountry/angola_34327.html.

UNITAG, U. 1989. "Namibia—UNITAG Background." UNSC Resolution. Accessed June 23, 2007. http://www.un.org/Depts/dpko/dpko/co_mission/untagFT.htm#Introduction.

UN (United Nations). 1948. "Universal Declaration of Human Rights, Adopted and proclaimed by General Assembly resolution 217 A (III) of 10 December 1948." Accessed August 02, 2007. http://www.un.org/Overview/rights.html.

———. 1949. "Universal Declaration of Human Rights." New York. United Nations Department of Public Information.

———. 1993. "Vienna declaration and Programme of Action." World Conference on Human Rights. Vianna, Office of the United Nations High Commissioner for Human Rights, Geneva.

———. 2002a. "The Millenium Development Goals and the United Nations Roles." Implementing the Millenium Declaration. Accessed August 01, 2007.

———. 2002b. "Plan of Implementation." World Summit on Sustainable Development. Johannesburg, United Nations. http://www.un.org/millenniumgoals/MDGs-FACTSHEET1.pdf.

UNDP (United Nations Development Programme). "Democratic Governance." Accessed April, 07, 2007. http://www.undp.org/governance/.

———. 1990. *Concept and Measurement of Human Development.* New York: Oxford University Press.

———. 1994. "Good Governance—And Sustainable Human Development." Accessed July 15, 2008. http://mirror.undp.org/magnet/policy/chapter1.htm.

———. 1994. "Govenance for Sustainable Human Development." http://gis.emro.who.int/HealthSystemObservatory/Workshops/WorkshopDocuments/Reference%20reading%20material/Literature%20on%20Governance/GOVERN~2.PDF.

———. 2000. *Human Rights and Human Development.* New York: Oxford University Press.

———. 2001. "Human Rights and Human Development." Human Development Report 2001. New York.

———. 2002a. *Deepening Democracy in a Fragmented World.* New York: Oxford University Press.

————. 2002b. "Public Financing of the Social Sectors in Angola." Accessed October 04, 2008. http://www.unicef.org/angola/ Financing_of_the_Public_sectors_in_Angola.pdf.

————. 2006. "Beyond Scarcity: Power, Poverty and Global Water Crisis." Human Development Report 2006. New York.

————. 2007. "Democratic Governance: Fostering Broad and Meaningful Participation." Annual Report. Geneva, United Nations Development Programme.

UNSC (United Nations Security Council). 1978. Resolution 435, "Namibia." September 29, 1978.

————. 1988. Resolution 626, Official Records of the Security Council, Forty-third Year, Supplement for October, November and December 1988.

————. 1991. Resolution 696. May 30.

————. 1992. Resolution 747. March 24. 1992.

————. 1993. Resolution 804. January 20.

————. 1993. Resolution 811. March 12.

————. 1993. Resolution 834 June 1.

————. 1994. Resolution 952. October 27.

————. 1994. Resolution 966. December 8.

United States Agency for International Development (USAID). 2005. Integrated Framework. Accessed April 04, 2012, http://pdf.usaid. gov/pdf_docs/PNADF423.pdf

VeneKlasen, L. 2004. *Rights-Based Approaches and Beyond: Challenges of Linking Rights and Participation*. Brighton: Institute of Development Studies.

Vines, A., N. Shaxson, L. Rimli, and C. Heymans. 2005. *Angola, Drivers of Change: An Overview*. London: Chatham House.

Ware, A. 1996. *Political Parties and Party Systems*. Oxford: Oxford University Press.

Webber, M. 1992. *Angola: Continuity and Change. Marxism's Retreat from Africa*. London: Frank Cass.

Weingast. 1997. "The Political Foundations of Democracy and the Rule of Law." *American Political Science Review* 91(2): 245-263.

Wepman, D. 1993. *Africa: The Struggle for Independence*. New York: Facts On File.

WHO 2003. "Right to Water. Health and Human Rights Publication Series." 3 Volumes.

WHO. 2006. "Angola: Core Health Indicators." Accessed August 4, 2007. http://www.who.int/whosis/database/core/core_select_process.cfm.

Wilson, F., N. Kanji, and E. Braathen. 2001. *Poverty Reduction: What Role for the State in Today's Globalized Economy?* London: Zed Books.

Windrich, E. 1994. "Media Coverage of the Angolan Elections." *Issue: A Journal of Opinion* 22(1): 19-23.

Wohlmuth, K. 1998. *Good Governance and Economic Development: New Foundations for Growth in Africa.* Bremen: Institut für Weltwirtschaft und Internationales Management, Universität Bremen.

Wolfers, M. 1979. *Poems from Angola.* London: Heinemann Educational.

World Bank. 1991. *Angola: An Introductory Economic Review.* Washington, D.C.: World Bank.

World Bank. 2008. "World Bank and Government of Angola Sign Second Phase of Recovery project (EMRP2)." Accessed September 2008, 2008. http://go.worldbank.org/1I9IVVO6V0.

World Movement for Democracy. Accessed September 14, 2007. http://www.wmd.org/about/information.html.

TABLE OF ILLUSTRATIONS

Figures

Tables